WHAT'S KEEPING YOU UP AT NIGHT?

Great Founders Ask Great Questions

KATIE LEWIS and MATTHEW STAFFORD

ISBN 978-1-80541-763-7 (eBook)
978-1-80541-764-4 (Paperback)

Published by 9others Ltd
www.9others.com

First published in 2025

WHAT'S KEEPING YOU UP AT NIGHT?

This is the most practical business book I've read in a long time 🤯

Just finished reading "What's keeping you up at night?"– highly recommended if you're entrepreneurial.

What Matthew Stafford and Katie Lewis have done is take insights from their 9others dinners with some of the smartest entrepreneurs in the UK and the world and share it in a direct do-this-then-do-that way.

Most how-to business books are very wishy-washy or just could have been a blog post . . . this isn't one of them.

10/10 book.

Get it. Thank me later.

– Timothy Armoo, Entrepreneur & Author

The meals with 9others were a great way to test feedback to what3words in the early days.

More than that, using the 9others network I was able to source talent and recruit early team members.

– Chris Sheldrick, Co-founder & CEO, what3words

I think the book is an INCREDIBLE resource for founders.

An invaluable book to help you grow your business from people who have founded, networked and invested in this space for many years.

Matthew and Katie have a lot of experience from years in their careers and hosting 9others meals with founders all over the world and they have distilled these lessons, as well as important questions for you to ask yourself as you start and scale up your business.

Highly recommended!

– Danielle Newnham, Founder, author & podcast host

Matthew Stafford and I have parallel lives. While he and Katie Lewis were building 9others, I was building VALUEx – my investment conference.

We all arrived at the same insight: Skip the big-stage conferences and go straight to small circles with strict confidentiality and blunt honesty. That's how businesses grow, lives change, and real work gets done.

In "What's Keeping You Up at Night?" Matthew and Katie strip all the fuss out of networking.

What's left? Nine others, some hard questions, and real answers. If you, like us, think that social capital is worth more than any balance sheet, you need to read this book – and start your own table of 9others.

– Guy Spier, Founder of the Aquamarine Fund & VALUEx

"What's Keeping You Up at Night? captures the magic of shared challenges and mutual support in the startup world. It's a must-read for any founder who's ever felt alone in the trenches – this book shows you how to find your people, ask for help, and build something extraordinary together.

– Laura Harnett, Founder & CEO of The Seep Company

Wonderful . . . The ultimate Personal Archive exercise for entrepreneurs – ten essential questions that invite reflection and will shape how you build, scale, and sustain your business.

— Matt Zeigler, founder of Cultish Creative

"What's Keeping You Up at Night?" doesn't try to romanticize the founder journey – it meets you where you are: in the uncertainty, the trade-offs, the 2 a.m. questions. It's a rare book that understands building a company isn't just about hustle – it's about reflection, resilience, and finding the right people to think alongside you. The right questions, asked in the right rooms, can change everything.

– Catherine Liao, Health tech builder and operator at Cardiex, Cisco, WHO, and University of Cambridge

Acknowledgements

Katie and Matthew would like to thank their families (for Katie: Nigel; and for Matthew: Jo, Olivia and Ted) for their support, as well as the incredible 9others community. A special thanks to Robbie Dale, who helped us bring this book to life.

Table of contents

The first time you bake cupcakes,
you will certainly follow the recipe with rigour.
Gaining confidence, by the third time,
you might improvise and screw up.
Learning your lesson, you will follow the recipe
again and again as closely as you can.
At this point, the fifth time,
some people actually learn to bake.
They improvise successfully.
They understand the science and the outcomes.
They develop a kind of gracefulness in the kitchen.
Others merely plod along.
They never experience the thrill of failing
or the generosity of creation.
They're cooks, not chefs.
We have too many cooks.
The world is begging for chefs.
Go, make work that matters.

– Seth Godin, The London Session, 2 November 2015

Preface to the Second Edition

When we first published 'Find your 9others' in July 2023 it marked ten years of bringing founders together around dinner tables around the world. We wrote it to thank the people who had joined us, shared openly, and helped each other through the real, raw challenges of building a business.

But something happened that we didn't expect.

The book spread. People started reading it who had never heard of 9others. It found its way to founders in the U.S., Southeast Asia, across Europe, and beyond. They recognised themselves in the stories. They told us they wished they'd found this kind of community sooner. We realised then that the message was bigger than the network. It was a message every entrepreneur needed to hear—wherever they were in the world.

So we decided to retitle the book for this second edition.

We chose *What's Keeping You Up at Night?* because that's the question we ask at every 9others meal. It's the invitation that kicks things off. It opens the door to honesty, to vulnerability, and to insight. Around that question, thousands of founders have shared their biggest challenges—and found support, perspective, and often, a way forward.

This book is about that moment.

It's about the power of asking better questions—of yourself, and of others. It's about realising that success in entrepreneurship doesn't come from pretending you've got it all figured out. It comes from seeking help, giving help, and surrounding yourself with people who are on a similar journey.

Though the content of the book hasn't changed much, our intent has. The first edition was written for those already in the room. This one is for anyone building something ambitious who needs a trusted space to ask the hard questions.

We believe now, more than ever, that your success will require the aid of others—and that the best way to get that help is to start by being helpful. This book offers stories, lessons, and the kinds of questions that have sparked breakthroughs for thousands of founders at 9others tables around the world.

Whether you're here for the first time, or returning for a second read, we hope this book prompts reflection, encourages action, and reminds you: you don't have to go it alone.

We'll leave you with the same question we always begin with.

What's keeping you up at night?

—Matthew & Katie
Co-founders of 9others

Introduction to what 9others is and how we started

The image of the hero founder is seductive. There they are – on the cover of a magazine, getting an award, in the headlines with millions or even billions next to their name. When starting out, first-time founders look at these people and wonder, *'Do I have what it takes? Can I do that?'*.

Entrepreneurship has come to be seen as the new rock 'n' roll. By the end of the 2010s *everyone* was an entrepreneur with a startup – or at least an idea for one. But when things look 'cool', when we see these heroes, we look up to them, and we're only told about the positives and the success stories, special powers, innate gifts, connections and luck the rest of us don't have.

But… but… what about when you're thinking of starting a startup, or you're in the thick of building one – how do you know if you're really cut out for it? (We'd hazard a guess that you're already questioning whether or not you are.)

If you're feeling like this, you're not alone. Since 2011 we've sat around the dinner table with thousands of founders in exactly the same situation you're in now. From our in-depth, trusted conversations with this incredibly diverse founders group we've learned some key insights that we can now share with you.

But how did that come about? Well, it all started back in 2011. We – Katie and Matthew – were both working in different investment companies in London. As fate would have it, we were brought together to work on a government-backed 'investment readiness programme' to support the startup scene in the city. It was a huge success. We were part of a brilliant team that helped hundreds of startups, and we saw dozens raise eight-figure funding. It felt amazing to be able to use our experience and passion to help others, and so, over the odd celebratory drink, we pondered if we could do more.

Our first step towards what would become 9others was running investor and founder dinners for these startups as part of that government programme. They worked well to network the groups and would prove successful in securing funding. But we quickly noticed that, at the end of each meal, not unlike a school disco, the investors and the founders would decamp to opposite sides of the room and not engage with each other. It was maddening! We'd got them there to talk to each other, and that wasn't happening.

It took us a few dinners, but we eventually realized what was going on. The founders were drawn to each other to discuss the everyday 'business of business' challenges that they were facing and struggling to discuss anywhere else. As such, learning from peers about the constant battering of cashflow, office space, hiring, firing and much else was deemed more valuable than connecting with investors – simply because it was such a scarce opportunity.

Usually, and you may recognize this, your life as a startup founder is spent in pitch mode. You know you need to look successful, full of energy and ready to take on the world. You want investors to buy into you, and, of course, partners and potential customers too. Which means that, at investment and networking events, there's no room for the things keeping you up at night. We spied an opportunity.

Sitting down to discuss it, we wondered what an event designed specifically for founders to talk about their biggest challenges would look like. We felt it would be best to keep it deliberately small, say ten people in total; it would be loosely curated so that everyone there would bring their own perspective and value to the group; and it would still be done over dinner because, well, that's never a bad thing.

And from there, 9others was born. For those not familiar with 9others, we run dinners with exactly ten people – you and nine others – in which every attendee is asked to give a brief introduction and table their biggest challenge: the answer to the question, *'What's keeping you up at night?'* That's it; one big question, ten potential answers. We then spend 10–15 minutes on each question, helping each other, before moving around the table. Simply put, if someone is willing to come along, share a challenge and help the others, then they get to go to dinner with nine other people willing to do the same.

But it doesn't end there. The dinner is the starting point for us to get to know everyone who attends, whom we can then welcome into our wider, global network. And it's a big network – the meals with 9others have happened 500+ times in 45+ cities and been attended by 5,000+ people. We've asked them all that same question: *'What's keeping you up at night?'* Therefore, this book is ultimately about the benefits that these opportunities can – and should – have for all founders in the hope that we can extend our reach even further.

We created 9others in this way because we could see the value that entrepreneurs can provide to each other; we could see the power of a network and the power of asking the right questions. Not just that it helps to know more people (everyone gets that), but that your success – however you define it – will absolutely require the aid of others.[1] We feel that so strongly, in fact, that it's our strapline: 'Your success requires the aid of others.'[1] We knew that if we connected good people, then they would go and make good things happen. We knew because it had happened to us, and we'd seen it happen whenever we'd brought groups of people together. So we wanted to formalize that in some way and make it a regular thing.

Now, over 13 and a half years since the first meal with 9others, 9others drives everything we do: Katie is the COO at Aspire, a high-growth scaleup, and has supported thousands of companies to raise investment in the UK and abroad. Matthew is a connector, investor and trusted counsel to entrepreneurs around the world.

When we meet people, as we develop relationships, we feed all that goodness back into the 9others network and watch great things happen. And because of our intimate connection, via the dinners, to everyone in that group, we're able to make connections of real value. We've forged many business partnerships, lots of investment, sales, hires and acquisitions, and, in one case, we've connected two people who served as bridesmaids at each other's weddings.

---

[1] S. Sinek, *Start with why: How great leaders inspire everyone to take action* (2011).

We decided to write this book to celebrate reaching ten years of 9others, with a few updates from the last few years in this 2nd edition. We believe our mission, our 'why', is so important that we hope we're still doing it in ten years' time, and indeed far longer. We often say that if we hit the jackpot with any investments, or indeed if anything goes horribly wrong, then we'll still find the time and space to host one 9others dinner each month. And at the end of the day, our hope is simply that 9others outlives us, and that the network exists to help people, solve business problems and create real success for as long as we're all still sitting down to eat dinner.

In *What's keeping you up at night?* you're getting raw insights from people who have been there and done it, and, more than that, most of whom are still doing it. This is not a book full of old millionaires reminiscing about the early days.

With this book, we've captured the things we've learned that are of real value to founders. We've observed thousands of conversations over the years, many of them very candid, open and detailed, and we hope you'll find as much value in them as we have.

Each chapter will discuss a question that our founders think is important to wrestle with. We illustrate this with founders' thoughts in a section called 'From the dinner table', where you'll hear from some of the most inspiring and ambitious founders who've been to 9others. And we finish with questions we want you to ask of yourself and others. We believe that answering these questions for yourself will give you the confidence to be bold, disciplined, ambitious and not afraid of being vulnerable as you go about building your business.

With questions 1, 2 and 3 we will help you focus on knowing who you are and what you want to build. Questions 4, 5, 6 and 7 will help you understand what you want and how you're going to get it. And questions 8, 9 and 10 are about how to go out there, build your network and ask for help.

Starting a startup is one of the most difficult things anyone can do. The people you'll read about have started, failed, tried again, given up, found their way again and achieved incredible success. So you'll read about the highs and the lows, but also about the opportunities they can offer to meet and work with some of the smartest and most inspiring people on the planet.

So how do they do it?

The answer to this, and many of the toughest questions, is actually very simple.

To be successful you need help.

And the best way to get help is to begin by helping other people. By starting a startup you'll be doing something difficult and something new. Most of the time there's no single correct answer, and you will be under huge pressure to make decisions and show leadership. There will be difficult conversations that will make you uncomfortable. You'll probably want to give up quite often, and you'll realize that you can't do all this alone. You'll need others.

You'll also need to trust your gut. Will you have the courage to? You'll need to be resilient, disciplined and brave. You'll also need to forge your own path and know what success means to you – it might not be what you think, and it might not be what you think others expect. You'll need a network, and you'll need to maintain it. You'll need to know who can help you and who you can help. You can't do all this on your own.

You might even find it useful to find your own 9others that you can help and can help you along the way. But to begin, you'll need to ask yourself a few questions...

Question 1
Why am I doing this, anyway?

This was something very personal to me, but that personal issue was felt by a sizable audience, and I realized there was a once-in-a- generation opportunity to build something with real purpose.

– Srin Madipalli, founder of Accomable

What is the not-so-secret sauce that helps founders? It's the 'why' of them. It's so straightforward, in fact, that you've no doubt been asked it before. And if not directly, then at least in books, podcasts and articles you've read. Well, I'm afraid we're here to add to the pressure. Because 'why you do what you do' is, we've found, the not-so-secret sauce that helps startups of all shapes and sizes get a real grip on their ambitions. If you can crisply and clearly articulate your 'why', then it's that much easier to know where you're heading, how to make the right decision for you and your business and how to attract others who want to work towards the same things you do. When you're faced with the harsh reality of running a startup, answering that question is not only going to make success likely; it will make it possible.

Don't panic if you find this question hard to answer, however – many do. But time spent working on your 'why' is time well spent.

Our why

In 2011, before founding 9others, both of us were meeting dozens of entrepreneurs each week. Some were incredibly clear about what they were doing, while others had a real hesitation; they simply didn't know *why* they were leaping into the void with their ideas. We spotted quickly that the gulf between the two was huge, and this was reflected in their ability to raise funding, sell their products, attract talent and, ultimately, be taken seriously. We therefore knew that if we wanted people to take us seriously, we'd need to be very clear on our 'why'.

To find it, we put some time in the diary and simply asked each other the question: 'Why are we doing this?' In this exercise, what we were really asking was 'why do we want to connect entrepreneurs to each other, and why do we think a dinner is a good way to do that?' because that was the idea we had for something that felt right. It's useful to get specific with these questions to get specific answers.

We thought it might take 30 minutes to jot down some useful answers, then we'd swiftly move on to practical conversations about scheduling, partners and so on. In the end, the 'why' conversation took all day.

We asked 'why?' a lot. We asked 'so what?' We asked each other to justify our answers. To generate something useful, it's important not to be shy about being open and honest, and to have the confidence in yourself and any co-founders to find your way to an answer that works for you. Skipping the tough parts will only cause more issues later.

For us, the breakthrough came after several hours when we hit upon a phrase we still use to this day: 'Your success requires the aid of others.' As soon as it landed in the conversation we both knew that was it. Indeed, it was so obvious to us that we didn't need to search any further; we simply wrote it on a whiteboard, took a photo and started packing up. Connecting entrepreneurs to others was our mission. Helping people understand that they needed those others to achieve success was why we were doing it.

Finding your why is like finding the love of your life: you just know.

Recognizing this in stripped-back, simple terms gave us real confidence that it was something we not only wanted to do but could also deliver against. And that confidence continued, and indeed grew, over many weeks, months and years as we presented this mission to people and had it well received. Or when it wasn't, we could see exactly why somebody didn't chime with our mission and understood that it wasn't our job to convince everyone, just to know that there was a tribe of others who wanted to come with us. And they did.

Be honest

You might consider it lucky that we landed on something that resonated with both of us so strongly. Indeed, if you're struggling to find cohesion on a mission in your own team, the nice, neat story we've just outlined here might feel frustrating. But the reality is, of course, that it wasn't luck. It was the product of both of us coming together with the same frustrations, the same beliefs and the same observations about the startup world we worked in every day. And although we couldn't articulate it when we first started talking about 9others, we had enough in common to sense that we were well matched to build something exciting. If that sense of electricity isn't already there, then coming up with a mission, and agreeing on why you're all doing whatever it is you're trying to do, is going to be hard. And the solution isn't likely to be trying harder, or talking longer; it's going to be accepting that you're not properly aligned, the solution to which may be changing your team.

Your 'why' is your guide, a compass always pointing in the direction you need to go. Whenever you're in doubt about what choices to make, you can check it and see where it points you. For us, we wrapped it into the name – 9others, i.e., it's about others, not just us. But even if you don't do that, you also need to think about ways to keep your mission clear in the minds of everyone working on it.

We've worked with thousands of entrepreneurs of all types and at all stages of business, and we can immediately tell when the individuals and teams we're talking to haven't done enough work on their 'why', because they themselves don't quite seem convinced. And it's always combined with a struggle for clarity in articulating the value proposition of the business, and the knock-on effect that has on attracting investment and talent. After all, why would potential investors or colleagues put up time, energy and money for something if the founders themselves can't say why they're really doing it?

Everything we've covered so far relates very directly to businesses and organizational missions, but what about personal missions? Why are *you* doing what you're doing? Why are you involving yourself in an organization and its mission? Maybe it's for money. Or fame. Or recognition. Or maybe it's something more purposeful; it doesn't really matter. All that matters, just as with the business mission, is being honest about what you're looking to get out of things for yourself. It's that honesty and that clarity which will allow you the smooth passage to success. And, of course, it's that honesty that ensures you are totally aligned with what you're trying to achieve; that you truly believe in the mission. If you're doing something because you think it's what you should do but don't really get why, then it won't work. And that's as true for 'making loads of money' as it is for 'tackling the climate crisis'.

Keep focused

When we started thinking about 9others, we made the common error of getting too caught up in what other people were doing. We were aware of First Tuesday, for example, a network that was built very quickly and then sold, and we wondered if we could do the same. We panicked about Grub With Us, a Y Combinator startup about to land in London. Both were dragging us towards big ideas of scale necessitating dozens of dinners each night with dozens of people, and that wasn't what we were trying to build. It's easy to get seduced by the success, scale and indeed money being achieved elsewhere, but you need to remember that each of those is the product (by and large) of a business having its own clear mission and sticking to it. It is the product of the founders having a clear mission for themselves that they can achieve through the business.

You can't go on someone else's mission and expect to succeed.

We believe that the power of 'why' is multiplicative. A personal mission is powerful, and a business mission is powerful. They needn't be exactly the same, but they should be in tune with each other so that, when put together, you get something significantly grander and more exciting than the sum of its parts. And it's this level of sheer energy that will give you the momentum to make it through the toughest of times.

Focus is just as important for knowing what not to do as for what you need to think about. Knowing our 'why' for 9others allowed us to say 'no' to things that just weren't aligned with what we were trying to achieve. And doing so meant we didn't get distracted by things that weren't adding value. Of course, it's hard to say 'no' to opportunities and offers, but it's much easier to rationalize when you can explain your decision in the context of your overriding mission. If the person offering you something understands what you're trying to do, and they believe in you enough to want to partner with you in the first place, then they'll understand. They might even be able to change their approach or suggest other people you can work with who will help you on your way. It's a win–win situation. Anyone can say 'yes' to please others; the valuable skill is knowing when to say 'no'.

To illustrate, it might be useful to look at some of the things we said 'no' to along the way and how we made those decisions.

People have always asked us if we offer discounts for 9others – sometimes because they're chancing their arm, sometimes because they don't quite believe in what we're offering. To them, and to everyone, we're always very clear that 9others is about contributing. We expect those who come to our dinners to contribute to the conversation, to the atmosphere and to the costs of running the event. It's something that has helped attract the right people and ensure everyone at the dinner is there under the same circumstances.

We've also regularly been asked by businesses if they can sponsor our 9others dinners, but this is something we found it easy to say 'no' to. At a 9others dinner, everyone around the table has an equal footing and can speak freely. If we had a sponsor in the room (who would surely expect some materials to be shared with our audience at the very least, even if they weren't there physically), then could our advice and input be taken seriously? Would it put off competitors of that sponsor from attending? Would we feel compelled to change what we do? Or simply stuff the room with warm bodies to ensure we ticked the box of running the dinner for the sponsor? We're very clear that success requires the aid of others, but we have never felt comfortable in that context taking additional aid from one particular source. Better, as described above, to let the attendees support each event and keep it focused on them.

We've sometimes said 'no' to people who wanted to come to events, people who we didn't feel were ready for 9others. That might be for many reasons, but it all comes back to this idea of contributing. If someone doesn't have any experience in business or expertise in a particular field that could add value to the conversation, then it's hard to rationalize their place at the table. As with the sponsors, we don't just want anybody who can pay the ticket price to attend. We want people who will form a valuable part of a peer-to-peer conversation. And for that they must bring experience, and their experiences, to the table.

Each of these 'rules' has helped us to keep 9others very streamlined and much simpler to operate. In turn, these 'rules' have given every dinner the best chance of success for everyone involved. That doesn't mean it was easy – in fact it was really hard, especially in the early days – to say 'no' to extra people and to sponsorship money. But it was important. And it was right for us.

From the dinner table

I've long been obsessed with the power of financial well-being and the power of money to create opportunity and choice. But I eventually realized that most people don't understand that power – or at least don't know how to wield it – and so I was spurred on to try and make a dent in this problem. I was lucky to be raised in a financially literate home where investments, risk and all manner of other financial topics were discussed at the table. It felt, and continues to feel, strange to me that other people don't have financial confidence. I wanted to change that. That was the mission I set out on. Jewish scripture tells us that we all (should!) carry two metaphorical pieces of paper in our pocket: the first tells us we are the centre of the universe, the second that we are insignificant. It's about balancing arrogance and humility, and I guess I really feel that. On the one hand, the problem is so big, so global and so seemingly intractable. On the other hand, if I don't do it, then who will? I think that is a real driver too.

– Vivi Friedgut, founder of Blackbullion

Starting Accomable was a bit of an accident. I'd been learning to code after finishing business school, as it seemed a good idea to develop those skills, but I needed something tangible to work on, so I thought: why not fix a problem I experience myself? I've been a wheelchair user my whole life and a couple of years earlier had taken six months off to travel. Accommodation was one of the many areas of accessibility that regularly failed to deliver for me. I booked so many places that said they had ramps, for example, but didn't! I'd be left scrambling in the middle of the night to find a solution or new accommodation. It was never easy. So I wondered if I could create a curated list of properly accessible, tried-and-tested accommodation that wheelchair users, and others, could use to ensure they could trust their holiday accommodation. It took off immediately once I put it out into the world. We had more demand than we knew what to do with, and way more demand than supply. It was clear that the community of wheelchair users was seriously neglected and underserved. With Airbnb, Uber, etc. all scaling and taking off, it was clear that we had the audience, and we were set up where there was real action. This was something very personal to me, but that personal issue was felt by a sizable audience, and I realized there was a once-in-a-generation opportunity to build something with real purpose.

– Srin Madipalli, founder of Accomable

Just because you love eating exquisite meals in excellent restaurants doesn't mean you want to be a chef.

I am very surprised at how many times people focus on the result of an activity but don't pay much attention to the process necessary to get there. Ultimately, the process is what you will be doing day in and day out, for months or years. I always suggest reflecting deeply on what the day-to-day process will be before making a big career decision, such as leaping into entrepreneurship.

My personal motivation is a mix of two things:

1. One thing I always hated in my previous jobs in advertising agencies was not knowing why I was doing something. I used to ask myself, 'Why am I doing this storyboard with 40 frames when it's clear that we need way less for this short advertisement film we are putting together?'

2. I genuinely like to help people and see them satisfied with my creative work. I want to focus on the quality of work to achieve success, not the quantity of work just for the sake of it. Doing it this way I, thankfully, got busy, so I ended up with more work than I could do on my own and asked others to help me.

These two forces combined resulted in me founding my own production studio. I never wanted to disappoint a client, and by building this culture I could surround myself with others who were aligned; therefore, the process was even more enjoyable. There's no better way to satisfy your curiosity than this!

– Stefano Marrone, visual storyteller

Conclusion

So there you have it. Question one, to go with nine others: you need to know why you're doing what you're doing. Not only will it help you focus on what you should do but also recognize what you shouldn't.

We've seen that the most ambitious founders are driven by something deeper. They're driven not (just) by scale or money, but by the impact they want to have on the world. This is what keeps them motivated when obstacles drop in their way, and it gives them the momentum they need to succeed, whatever the world throws at them.

You need your version, too, to give you the best chance of succeeding. That's simply because the outcome of knowing your 'why' is no longer having to worry about what's driving the business. You're not wasting time and energy wondering if you're doing the right things; you're spending time and energy focused on the things that will actually help you fulfil your mission and grow.

Your 'why' is the solid platform your success is built on.

Questions to ask of yourself and others

Not quite sure of your 'why' yet? Don't panic. These simple questions can help you better understand your mission.

Why am I doing what I'm doing? Ask yourself this and, when you have an answer, ask yourself 'why' again. Several times if needed. Ask 'why' until you can't ask 'why' anymore. What you will find at the end of that journey will be a clear mission. It can be a good idea to do this with a trusted friend or colleague who can really hold you to account.

What am I doing this for? Are you seeking external validation? Warren Buffett has some wise words to share here: 'Would you rather be the world's greatest lover, but have everyone think you're the world's worst lover? Or would you rather be the world's worst lover but have everyone think you're the world's greatest lover?'[2]

What do I really want? Is it fame, money, awards, self-satisfaction? Any of these things are perfectly fine, but you need to know what it is *for you* and *for your business*, and the most ambitious have something deeper.

How do I use my time? You can work out if the mission you've landed on really is 'the one' by looking at what you actually do with your time. For example, do you stay up late working on this mission? Does it occupy your mind on the weekends, outside of traditional working time? Or would you rather watch TV, sleep or do a hobby than think about your supposed mission? If you would, then it's not your 'why'. If you have to force yourself to find the time and energy to commit to a mission, then you're already struggling before you begin.

---

[2] A. Schroeder, *The snowball: Warren Buffett and the business of life* (2009).

Question 2
How do I get more visible?

> *In the early days we had very little to show potential clients by way of previous work, so generating that visibility ourselves was a must. Elevating my profile was essentially a way to show brands that we could do this.*
>
> – Timothy Armoo, founder of Fanbytes

Why should anybody pay you any attention? It's a blunt but important question, and one you absolutely need to be able to answer – not least because it's the one that investors and customers are always asking. Fortunately, it follows on very neatly from understanding your own 'why', so we'll make use of that momentum.

Be visible

Being visible takes courage. There's risk. You'll open yourself up to criticism, rejection, pressure.

As discussed in Question 1, your mission should energize you and keep you focused on what's important as you tackle the myriad challenges that startup life will throw at you. But it also does something else: it acts as a beacon to those who will help make your business a success. It makes you visible.

Marketing sage Seth Godin made a pithy observation back in 2012: 'You will be judged, or you will be ignored'.[3] And since you don't want to be ignored, you better get comfortable being judged. It is, of course, uncomfortable being judged, even if the judgement is ultimately positive, but it is utterly necessary. Without judgement, how could anybody decide if they wanted to buy from you, or partner with you, or work for you?

We're all making judgements all day, every day, and they ultimately guide our choices. That's because we are all in search of something, be that solutions, meaning, peace or something else. This, in turn, means we're all on a constant lookout for the people, projects, artworks – and, of course, businesses – that can bring us such solace. Therefore, to stand out in this world you need to present yourself clearly as a gathering point for like-minded people. And to do that, you need to send a very clear signal to the world about who you are, why you exist and, by extension, why people should care about you.

If knowing your 'why' helps you focus on the right things, then acknowledging and embracing the need to be visible – and vulnerable to judgement – is what helps you translate a mission into action that will make real waves.

Take action. Try something. Put yourself out there.

---

[3] S. Godin, *You will be judged (or you will be ignored)*, Seth's blog (2012). Available from: https://seths.blog/2012/05/you-will-be-judged-or-you-will-be-ignored/

Don't be bland

On discovering 9others for the first time, people often tell us that they like what we're doing. This is, of course, lovely to hear. And it shows that the vision we have appeals to people who aren't us. Which is handy, as any success we've had since 2011 is entirely down to our idea resonating with a constant stream of diner-cum-networkers who see value in what we're doing.

But it's also interesting to dig a little further into these comments, as what comes out of people's mouths next unerringly falls into two camps. Camp one is home to the people who buy into our vision completely. They like the dinner set-up, the limitation to ten people around a table, the focus on solving challenges and the energy we're adding into the startup scene in general. They seem to take comfort from the fact that 9others exists and connects with their vision of the world.

The second group are those with 'advice'. Those who believe in the broad value of networking, sure, but who think our very specific limitation of ten people is frankly crazy. Or who wonder if one-to-one networking is a better approach. Or speed networking drinks. Or subject-specific webinars that are not limited by geography. Or a club dedicated to networking and growth through the ancient art of bonsai.

The thing is, both groups prove the point we're making in this chapter: putting yourself out there helps you find your tribe. Because we put ourselves out there – we hosted the first few meals in a way that aligned with our 'why' – some people were drawn to that; they embraced it. For others, they saw 9others and it didn't quite fit their view of the world. Of course, both are okay. Both are, in fact, needed. To paraphrase Seth Godin's point, if you're too bland to annoy anyone, you're also too bland to engage them. And that means you're forever destined to dine alone.

Don't be put off by the naysayers

In July 2012 we decided to take the 9others concept beyond the confines of London and out to sunny Barcelona. We reached out to our relatively small network at that stage (75 people or so) and were introduced to three people out in Spain. Excited, we promptly set up discussions to share our vision and, we hoped, get some support. But the first two people we spoke to just didn't get what we were trying to do. In fact, they gave us conflicting opinions on why 9others wouldn't work in Barcelona: 'It's too big a place,' said one, while the other told us the city was just too small! Adding confusion to injury, we were told that there was too much going on to get cut-through, but also that the landscape was very quiet and we'd struggle to convince people to come to an event like ours. It was both dispiriting and frustrating.

That was until we met Elise. Elise instantly 'got' 9others. In fact, before we'd even finished explaining what we were doing and what we wanted to do in Barcelona she ran ahead of us, describing 9others back to us in her own terms and excitedly reeling off people she could invite and cafés she could charm into hosting.

The lesson? Don't be put off by the naysayers who can't help you achieve your vision. Even if they think they're being helpful, the only possible outcome of their involvement is to derail your efforts. Put them to one side, don't let them knock your confidence and focus on those who get what you do. They're the ones who will support your success (as long as there's enough of them, of course[4]). Focusing on the Elises of the world has seen us host dinners in more than 45 cities across the globe, and our experience with Elise – and others – helped us to quickly assess potential hosts so we could stay positive and keep moving forward. And that all comes from us putting ourselves out there and knowing from sheer effort and experience that if someone doesn't like it… someone else will.

Let's get visible

When you come up with a brilliant idea for a business, it's tempting to want to dive straight in and start putting it under people's noses. This urge is even more appealing when you see others with similar ideas already reaping the rewards of customers, coverage and cash.

You need to focus on a way to be visible that is authentic to you and your business.

The good news is that visibility can be achieved in several different ways, which means you can put yourself out there in a style that suits you. For 9others, for example, our visibility has come in a number of ways (some of which we have relished and some we've found much harder).

The first thing people latch on to is our name, and people tend to like it. '9others' means something, as it encapsulates what we do. It instantly invites people into our simple vision of dinners with like-minded people, and it helps that it often gets listed first alphabetically on attendee lists at networking events and the like. It visually stands out from many other names.

---

[4] We're taking as read that you need a big enough market to support your business. For some that's just a handful of people, for others it's 100,000s. Whichever it is, the principles remain.

However, a nice name is just a tiny piece of the puzzle. We've had to take the vision and present it far and wide to get to where we are today. At the start this meant being incredibly proactive by going to networking events, handing out business cards,[5] having follow-up meetings over coffee, putting ourselves forward to talk at events and startup groups and getting in touch with anyone we'd ever met who we thought might be interested. The energy we put in here has really paid off in the long run, but, of course, each of these approaches has its own hurdles.

With the low-level grind of sending emails, the hurdle is the boredom. It feels as if you're contacting people with the same info, often not getting a response, and as if you've spent a whole afternoon not really achieving much. But that isn't true. First, putting your vision in front of people isn't a one-off task, and people don't respond for lots of reasons. So those contacts were simply the first step on a journey with all those people, some of whom have become huge supporters of 9others over the years. Second, it's an exercise in proving your commitment to becoming visible. Boredom aside, if you can't actually be bothered to send the first 1,000 individual emails introducing people to what you do, then it may not be worth you doing it.

One thing that's really helped our visibility is 9others' inclusion in various articles, podcasts, events and even books[6] as an example of best practice.

---

[5] Top tip: we put both of our names and numbers on these cards, which saved time setting them up, saved money and made them stand out a little more while also promoting a sense of inclusiveness.

[6] R. Koch, *The 80/20 principle: Achieve more with less* (2022). B. Evans, *How to Have a Happy Hustle* (2019) and T Mauri, 3D Leader (2020).

With public speaking it was, quite simply, the fear. Matthew doesn't particularly like public speaking but found himself with opportunities that were simply too good to ignore (i.e., the result was worth the price). The simple equation here is what tips the balance. And again, if you really believe in your vision, then the desire to share it, to help more people and to build something you believe in should easily trump the fear. For Matthew it did, and he found himself not only on stage with Seth Godin in 2013 talking about 9others but also standing up in front of audiences of hundreds at Imperial College and the like. The fear was ultimately a price worth paying. And, of course, it was never as awful as his imagination would have him believe.

Creating visibility takes time: time away from family and friends, time away from working on 9others and hosting more dinners, time away from other work commitments (or rather, time that means those work commitments need to be squeezed in elsewhere). That's the reality, of course. There are only 24 hours in a day. But, as we've noted already, how you use those hours tells you more about whether you're really committed to becoming visible.

Do *your* thing

Throughout this book we'll take the time to explore what our advice means for individuals as well as their businesses. After all, when you're the founder of something new, and you're working hard to bring that vision to life, it's as much about what *you* do.

Everyone we admire has done something to become visible. This doesn't mean they've become famous or recognizable to the masses; it simply means they are clearly visible to us. And each person who's visible in your universe has done something different to stand out. Some will, of course, be international superstars, some will be legends in a particular area, and some will be your friends and family. But whoever they are, and whatever it is that has made them visible, they were almost certainly nervous about what lay ahead when they first started out in the world – because that's totally and utterly normal.

The thing is, as a person, there's not the buffer of a company structure or a brand name to hide behind when you're building a startup. It really is just you. And if you put yourself out there, you will be vulnerable. However, it is critical to your visibility and therefore to your success. So if you want to make it, then you're going to have to get comfortable in the limelight.

Another way to look at this is that to make your vision visible, you'll need to show leadership. After all, it's your role to drag people with you and to rewrite the rules of how things are done. Indeed, we like to think of leadership as follows: when a new business is formed, it should exist to support a new way of doing things. As such, it also creates 'new rules of the game'. To attract players to this game, there are rules that need to be followed. As a leader, you set those rules, you enforce them and you make sure they deliver some value to everyone involved.[7]

And, of course, you're doing all this from scratch, so it's incredibly hard. But it absolutely can be done, and we've observed some useful ways that leaders have brought their vision to life over the years that may inspire you.

---

7 You can see our rules for 9others in Question 5, 'What does it take to succeed?'.

Pride in your people

The only truly unique thing about any business (other than certain kinds of intellectual property (IP), which is only relevant in very particular cases) is the people who are in that business. Leaders who understand this also understand that they need their people to help the vision become visible. This means involving them in thought processes and decision-making and leaning on them in the right ways. The best leaders really know how to delegate.

Know your audience

At different stages of your business you'll be talking to different audiences. To bring them with you and engage them with your vision, you will need to lead the people in front of you at that given moment. This might be your staff, investors, users, clients, partners or someone else. And it might be one-to-one or it might be millions (i.e., in your audience or in advertising). Adjusting your tone and approach to the people you hope to lead is important.

Ask for help

It's easy to assume that, just because you're the founder, you need to know everything. It is, as they say, lonely at the top. But this is an unrealistic expectation. Your success, as we say, very much requires the aid of others. It's part of why 9others exists, but it's also something that the best leaders instinctively understand. You have to get comfortable with seeking help when you need it so that you have the time and energy for the things you must do on your own as the founder and lead visionary.

Do the right thing

The best leaders always do the right thing. Mostly this means that they're nice, genuine people who are trying to make a real difference. That's not to say there aren't successful, unpleasant people – of course there are, but to achieve that they're going to need an absolutely scintillating vision[8] – or that you must be infallible. Stress, difference of opinion and plain old mistakes can make founders appear difficult or harsh, but you should always try to do right by your customers, staff and others whom you interact with. And you should always make sure your actions lead back to your values, or 'golden rules', and that everyone is clear on what these are.

From the dinner table

> *I think of visibility as a superpower. Fortunately it turns out that being visible is something I really enjoy. The PR, the speaking, the writing, the putting myself out there. I like it, and that's been really helpful for the business. After all, in the early days we had very little to show potential clients by way of previous work, so generating that visibility ourselves was a must. Elevating my profile was essentially a way to show brands that we could do this, that we knew how to be visible! More recently, however, I've found that even though we don't need to convince clients in the same way, I can use this superpower to*

---

8 By all reports, the famously difficult Apple founder Steve Jobs was not a nice person to work around a lot of the time, but he was always consistent with his approach to creating incredible products with an obsession for detail. He also treated everyone in the same way. If you bought into that vision and wanted to do the same, you could argue that the roller coaster was worth it. And you could ask if it is 'right', or even nice, to let people produce sub-standard work and disappoint customers just to avoid an argument?

inspire other founders, especially those with the same background as me, to get out there and achieve amazing things.

– Timothy Armoo, founder of Fanbytes

I've changed my path from being an entrepreneur to a venture capitalist. Therefore I'm in the business of elevating other entrepreneurs and those considering this path. As well as entrepreneurship I want to open up venture capital as a career path. There are no shortcuts; I've had to go out and build, learn, fail and get back up.

When I started as a VC I felt as if I was starting from scratch, and I knew I needed to find others. A few friendly female VCs invited me to events and WhatsApp groups to start to get me integrated. They were often newbies themselves or had been founders or operators before.

To speed things up in what's quite a closed industry I started to build my own community of diverse VCs and allies in FutureWorldVC.com and held educational and social events on topics I wanted to learn about. The key thing was to create a safe space where people could be open with each other about their gripes and a place where we could celebrate the wins together.

When I was an entrepreneur, I believed that having a strong personal brand gave me a bit of an advantage, so as a VC I've developed this too via social media, LinkedIn and Medium in particular.

My goal as an early stage VC is to find the best impact founders in Europe and invest impact capital, time, knowledge and networks so that they can build the next global, world-changing healthcare, education and climate technology companies. Putting myself out there, even when I was new to VC, has helped to raise awareness so that founders research me easily. Ultimately this helps me attract great deal flow, attract great co-investors and find senior executive talent to assist in the building of the most impactful companies.

– Zoe Peden, VC partner at Ananda Impact Ventures

A friend and I were discussing ways for me, as a founder up in Manchester, to be more visible in the tech startup ecosystems.

My first business was bootstrapped and had an international client base – it was really successful, but for that business I'd never really needed a network or community that was local to Manchester. In 2015 I was fundraising for Twine, and it was in that discussion with the friend that he said getting investor introductions from other founders was the most effective and authentic way to connect with investors. And what better way to be connected to more founders than to be the middle node in a good network?

I think the concept of 9others works really well for my personality. A small, intimate dinner is not overwhelming, everyone opens up, and I enjoy making others feel comfortable discussing their challenges. This works for me, and I'd encourage other founders to explore and find their own.

And, of course, being that middle node of the network has not only meant being visible but also that I've probably learned the most. It takes a lot of effort to put myself out there being a host, and it's something I take really seriously, but every time without fail I am just so pleased I did it.

– Stuart Logan, CEO at Twine AI and 9others host, Manchester

I moved up to Manchester from London in 2015 and knew that I needed to get in front of people.

I love networking in general and know that being visible is great for business, so it's something I've consciously worked on – I've been Chair of BIMA [British Interactive Media Association] and hosted loads of dinners and events for JB Cole and our clients. There's something different about 9others, though – I feel it's now an integral part of the Manchester scene, and Stuart and I have become known for all the right reasons.

There's just a kind of rawness and authenticity to 9others. Many networking events are about bravado, but the best thing is actually to show vulnerability. That sparks something in other people, and they think, 'You know what, I can help.'

– Josh Bolland, CEO and founder of JB Cole UK and 9others host, Manchester

Conclusion

Lesson two, then, is to put yourself out there. Get comfortable putting your head above the parapet and understand that it's normally a long slog getting noticed, but it's worth all those days (and weeks, and months) of feeling uncomfortable and as if you're treading water.

You're never going to inspire colleagues or wow customers, investors or the media with your take on things if you won't shout about it. And you can't expect clients, partners and supporters to go wild for what you have to offer if you can't be your first, very enthusiastic cheerleader.

Bringing your vision to the world requires you to step out of the shadows and shine.

Questions to ask of yourself and others

Hopefully you're now convinced of the importance of visibility. But to be seen more clearly, what kind of questions should you be asking yourself?

What are you going to do to become visible, and to whom? There are many ways that founders can become visible for the good of their business. Think about the ways that will suit your personality, but also realize that, whoever you are, it may feel uncomfortable in the beginning and not everything you try will work. You need to push through this to find the frameworks that allow you to connect with, and be seen by, the right people.

Is what I'm doing a version of what's come before? You're not going to stand out if you appear to be something people have seen in the past. Of course, everything is inspired by something, and we're all 'standing on the shoulders of giants', but be honest with yourself: are you a tribute act or are you promoting something original?

What do my customers care about? Am I trying to please everyone? Asking these two questions will help you get an external viewpoint on how your vision appears to others. It's commonly the case that early adopters in your space will instinctively recognize what you're trying to do, but there will be many, many more who don't. This may be fine at the start of your journey, but as you look to grow, mature and secure mass adoption, you'll need to be clear on why you're different, what's of value and who you're really trying to target.

What action are you going to take today? Try something, experiment. Look at a founder you admire. Is there one thing they do to be visible that you can try, even on a small scale? Put yourself out there.

Question 3
What do I do with my gut reactions?

In making that tough decision – some of it with my heart, some my head – I was content that I had given it my all.

– Seena Rejal

Yes, that's right; it's 'simple question time' again, and this time we're here to ask: can you put your gut feelings into words?

We've all been there. You feel something deep in your being that you know absolutely to be the case – that this thing will work or that person doesn't quite have what it takes – but, when asked why, you're either lost for words or end up saying far too many.

Gut feelings are important at 9others dinners. Often, when a challenge is tabled, the advice that rebounds is conflicting. This is to be expected. We always recall the example of an attendee who came to a dinner and asked if she should fire her first employee. Half thought she should, half thought she shouldn't! Not terribly helpful, except each had their reasons. The structure of a 9others dinner allows those reasons time to breathe, and it gives the guest asking for advice time to let it all settle in their gut.

People come from different places, with different experiences, different values and different perspectives on the challenge at hand. This is where the gut comes in. Those who have asked a question listen to the proposed answers and, if they're fortunate, find one that fits – one that settles comfortably in their gut in place of something they were missing. It's not necessarily to do with what's practical – or what's logical, of course. It's simply to do with what's right for them. Building on questions one and two, this largely means what fits with their 'why' and what works with building their visibility.

And while at a 9others dinner it's often enough to nod, smile and communicate thanks for the input as the discussion moves on, in most other contexts it would be rather useful to put that gut feeling into words. It helps give a tighter brief to those you ask for help in the future, and it helps communicate effectively with staff, investors and partners.

So this chapter will explore not just why you should trust your gut, but how you give it a voice.

Trust your gut

Real innovations are rarely reached by committee. Instead, the basis of something that rewrites the rules tends to arrive – as if from nowhere – in the mind of an individual. And when the idea is something that, to the originator at least, has real merit and demands exploration, the idea inevitably steps out of the head, takes a deep breath and launches itself with real weight and purpose into the gut. This is a great feeling. It breathes real life into us as individuals and can drive us forward with real intent. But let's be clear on something else too: none of this matters to other people. Unless you're a seasoned guru with success after success behind you, you can't really tell a customer, employee or investor to trust you simply because you feel something in your gut. Instead, you need to articulate what you're feeling.

The first step to giving your gut a voice is to understand what your gut is telling you, and this is best done by acknowledging what your gut can and can't do. It is not a sophisticated decision-making centre capable of analysing lots of information to come up with a slick answer to every question in every circumstance, so don't use it like that. What it can do is tell you if you're deviating off course or heading in the right direction.

This means you can trust your gut for your 'why' and the vision you've set out, but you need to look elsewhere when it comes to execution. If you can remember this, you will really harness the power of your gut feelings without damaging your business.

Too often we've seen founders get lost in 'product spin' – an obsession with the details of what they're building that drags them further and further from their vision. Instead, the most successful founders seem to understand that, while others can crunch the details, they are the only possible pilots of their vision. Therefore, this is where they need to be – leading the vision – lest everything crash in a fiery mess.

Your role as a founder is to bring your gut to important conversations so you can determine if a practical suggestion or specific feature idea feels right. It's that simple. And it's just as true whether talking with your own team or with particularly chatty people at parties.

We talked in the last chapter about the importance of putting yourself out there to be judged, and we acknowledged that this can be a scary prospect. With a clear sense of why you're doing what you're doing, however, even the worst feedback is put into perspective. Your actual customer profile is going to be the most important to listen to if you want them to actually buy what you're selling. Customer feedback can be brutal, but it's a lot easier to let the useless stuff go, and to see the useful stuff as genuinely helpful, if you put it through the filter of your gut.

We've trusted our guts a lot when it comes to 9others. By sticking to the vision that we wanted to achieve, we've been able to build something we're really proud of and find a tribe of people who buy into it too. As we've already touched on, there are other models of hosting dinners that aren't for us. So any proposed ideas from outsiders – no matter how experienced they are or how smart we've found them to be – that moved us away from our particular vision and towards something else was something our gut said 'no' to (and that has included writing a book before we had done the hard yards and had something to say).

Not only that, but the *more* people who questioned what we were doing or suggested different ways of approaching networking events and advice-sharing communities for startups, the more our guts learned and developed. You see, all these people sharing their opinions and offering their insights are incredibly useful because you can use them to hone and refine your sensitivity to exactly what it is you're trying to achieve in your work.

One of the best things about 9others is the sheer volume of ideas and information that gets thrown your way. Having attended hundreds of dinners, the matrix of challenges around any given table, and the dozens of different colliding opinions that are tossed around, is quite electrifying. It's embracing this reality that marks out the founders who get the most from our dinners (and, we think, everything else in startup life).

We've observed thousands of founders at hundreds of dinners, and those looking for a right answer are always disappointed. Largely because there are no simple answers to useful questions, but also because it suggests they haven't yet got in touch with their gut to hear what it's trying to say, which is probably something like, 'Listen and note what you hear from people when you discuss your vision; I'll do the rest.'

Back in 2012 Brian Taylor, co-founder of PixelPin, called 9others 'group therapy for startups', which, while subtle, is brilliantly accurate. What 9others does – and what we believe any good sounding board for founders should do – is provide a safe place where people can both listen and be listened to. Somewhere they can learn and unlock what's already inside them and build the courage they need to make effective decisions by listening to their gut.

Putting it into words

We promised up front that this chapter would help you take those indescribable gut feelings and give you a way to put them into words. Now that we've given some life and soul to the humble gut feeling, hopefully you'll see where we're coming from when we share these suggestions from our own experience.

The first thing we learned about giving our gut a voice was when we were forced to write the 'Golden Rules' of 9others.[9] This wasn't something we'd planned to do, but it became necessary when we needed to communicate our approach to everything to our very first overseas host in Barcelona. It forced us to find ways to put into words some of the instinctive rules we'd been following, sometimes without even noticing.

To do this, of course, we sat down and thought about the key elements that go into devising and running a dinner. But we also looked to our dinner guests to get a sense of the things they found important and to borrow their words in describing what they like about 9others. We had been gathering this through email feedback already and took the opportunity to start asking people in person.

An interesting side effect of this enforced exercise was that it led us to sketch out a kind of informal manifesto for 9others and ourselves. In doing this, we noticed that a lot of the things we – Katie and Matthew – had talked about for years and years together (or more often moaned about), and therefore had put into words, were the things that had formed the real essence of our gut feelings.

In practice, our gut feelings are simply reactions to the things we like, the things we don't like, the things that excite us and the things that make us feel sad. Since we can already talk about these things and describe them – to some extent, at least – we have a starting point for articulating our gut feelings. However, the main way we've given a voice to our gut on an everyday level is in developing what we call the '65% rule'.

---

9 You can see our rules in all their glory in Question 5, 'What does it take to succeed?'

The 65% rule is simple: if we're at least 65% sure of something, we do it. It acknowledges that we can never be 100% sure of something while allowing us to keep forward momentum. It also puts a measurement on things that are clearly better than 50:50, which speeds up decision-making and allows us to keep testing and learning without panicking too much.

Of course, 65% is an arbitrary and impossible-to-measure number, but it is something that we've found resonates with people. It means 'are you basically convinced this is a good idea but have some (understandable) reservations?', which, in turn, means you can take a deep breath and give it a go with suitable planning and risk assessment. If you're a natural at maths, you'll also notice this is close to saying that you feel something is twice as likely to go right (two-thirds) as it is to go wrong (one-third).

The thing to always keep in mind is the complex, irrational and illogical nature of success and, well, life: when we try to rationalize things too much, at best we end up missing the nuance of what makes things work, and at worst we completely sanitize the things we care about of any useful meaning whatsoever. So when we say you need to trust your gut, it's fundamentally about using your gut as part of the toolkit that guides you while keeping your wits about you as you go.

Trusting your gut is about having the confidence to know that the things you feel, and the things you instinctively know to be true, are actually built on the signals you've received from the rest of the world (i.e., through your experience, your experiments and the input of others). It is this confidence that what will get you to the 65% so you can keep moving forward.

From the dinner table

My first business, ETHOS, was a meat-free restaurant that launched in 2014. This was still a time when the word 'vegan' was a very dirty word. You would never openly admit in polite society that you were a vegan. I spoke to a consultant soon after launching ETHOS, and she told me that, in order to appeal to more customers, I needed to add fish to the menu. She had been a consultant at Pret A Manger, and I was just starting out on my journey at the time. I remember coming away from that meeting feeling really upset. She just didn't get it. Of course I never wavered – it was out of the question in my mind to add fish or any kind of meat. The whole point of ETHOS was to gently show people that they wouldn't even miss meat/fish when they ate with us.

– Jessica Kruger, ETHOS

Gut reactions are one way in which our intuition tries to get our attention. By intuition, I mean 'immediate insight without reasoning'. Intuition isn't based on 'fuzzy thinking' or 'touchy-feely' thinking, so we can be deliberate in listening to it. Intuition happens in the gap between thoughts, which is why many people who practise some form of silent meditation notice that their intuition becomes stronger and stronger as the gap between thoughts becomes longer and longer. To put it simply, flashes of inspiration have more chance of getting through when your mind is quiet.

However – and this is a big 'however' – there is such a thing as 'false intuition'. This is when painful experiences from the past distort your perception of what's happening now. It's widely accepted that experiences from our early childhood shape our reactions and behaviour for many years – perhaps the rest of our lives. It can be an apparently minor incident that sets this process in motion. To take a simple example, imagine that you're five years old and one of your parents refuses to buy you an ice cream. You're extremely upset, but you suppress the emotion instead of experiencing it from beginning to end. You come to the conclusion that 'life doesn't give me what I want'. Unless you do something to remove it, this cognition about life and other people will lead to disappointment over and over again. It's like a computer running a software program that keeps producing the opposite result to what you want.

I have learned a technique from Sri Nithyananda Paramashivam, known to his followers as Swamiji, that removes painful matters and prevents false intuition.

It's difficult and takes practise, but once you get rid of false intuition you're left with genuine intuition, which is based on love, not fear.

The ultimate stage is to let go completely, otherwise known as surrender. As Swamiji puts it, 'If you surrender, your intuition will tell you what to do… Surrender is enlightenment. Then you will know the truth.'

– John Purkiss, partner at August Leadership
and author of *The Power of Letting Go*

Stepping away from a company I had spent so many years building was a very difficult decision indeed. That decision was part gut, part logic, and here's how I thought about the process that took place.

I had spent many years developing the 3D search concept and business. However, a year after raising our seed round, we made a big pivot towards advanced video analytics with some new groundbreaking AI technology. (That, in itself, is a story for another time!)

We were pushing to raise the Series A round. It had become protracted. However, having won a leading international computer vision/AI competition, many new doors had opened to us, particularly in the US.

At last, we were settling into a clear product proposition with the new tech – advanced video analytics for online content moderation.

I had a great team, fantastic technology and, now, a clear product. Recurring revenue seemed at hand, making fundraising less pressing and improving our position vis-à-vis investors in negotiations.

Then Covid hit! Our discussions with potential clients and near-term revenue opportunities quickly dissipated. We did attempt to do a mini-pivot to capitalize on the Covid situation – the sudden focus on social distancing and human behaviours such as coughing were a great fit with our video analytics technology. We launched a platform to monitor this in public and private spaces as a way to help offices reopen and shops and common spaces to remain safe while in operation. Coverage of the solution by the BBC's 'Click' programme was a boon, but most potential clients sat tight and decided they were going to hold out for the pandemic to pass and so nothing came of that.

The lockdowns and isolation were a time for reflection for me. I came to the conclusion that the company, as it stood, had morphed into something that may eventually not become what I wanted it to, and that I no longer had the fire in my gut for the enterprise. The right thing for the company, the team and the investors – as well as for me – was to hand over the reins to someone else and begin anew. It was a clear decision to me, so the sooner I acted on it, the better.

In making that tough decision – some of it with my heart, some my head – I was content that I had given it my all. There is a difference between pushing hard against the odds – believing and never giving in – and deciding to make a change when it is no longer viable in the existing form and context. There is a line at which pushing on despite all evidence and signs turns from being courageously single-minded to being naively unaccepting and self-destructive. I didn't want that line to be crossed! There was no need to sink a ship and go down with it! Let the ship float on, in my case with a new team, which is best for them and will let me go and build a new, larger vehicle!

– Seena Rejal

Conclusion

Your gut is a very powerful tool if you understand how to use it.

Your gut is the compass that will tell you if you're on the right path; that's the simple bit. But it's a compass that needs refining and training. Open yourself to input (good and bad!), do more, experience more and talk to more people. And as you do, let your gut respond – and listen when it does. You may not have much idea what it's telling you to begin with, but as you take further action – and refer to what your gut told you to do – you'll start to get a sense of what 'right' feels like. Once you can more accurately measure that (for us it's the 65% rule), you can more accurately articulate your gut feelings to yourself and others.

Forward momentum comes from the confidence to trust your gut feelings, and that can be helped by putting them into words – by talking, and writing, about what you feel.

Questions to ask of yourself and others

What is my '65% rule'? Derek Sivers says, 'If it's not a "hell yes!" then it's a no.'[10] Maybe that's a bit extreme – indeed we think it is, hence 65% not 100% – but what feels right to you?

Who are my confidantes? These are people you can speak to in order to get honest, candid advice. People who will really tell you if something is a good idea or not, and why.

---

[10] D. Sivers, *Hell yeah or no: What's worth doing* (2022).

Can you develop a steel man argument? If you're unsure about a decision and your gut fighting with your external sources of information is leaving you floundering, you can find a way forward with a 'steel man argument'. This is the opposite of the 'straw man argument' you may be familiar with, whereby you argue against something based on false premises. With the 'steel man argument', you actively seek to make an argument as strong as possible. For example, if your customers are all telling you to do something but your gut is resisting it, take time to 'steel man'[11] the customers' point of view, i.e., make their argument as strong as possible. By doing this you should be able to explicitly identify what it is about the point of view that doesn't work for you and why you don't want to do it. If it's for a good reason (e.g., it's counter to your whole worldview), then that's useful. If it's for a bad reason (e.g., you're being a bit lazy), then that's useful too. And if you can't find an issue with the argument at all, then you need to decide if your gut is meeting your own 65% rule.

[11] The idea is outlined in R. Holiday, *Conspiracy: Peter Thiel, Hulk Hogan, Gawker, and the anatomy of intrigue* (2018).

Question 4
How do I keep getting up again?

Your courage starts flourishing the day you realize no one is coming to save you.

– Unknown

Simple question number four: what do you do when you get knocked down?

If (in the immortal words of '90s anarcho-pop band Chumbawamba) you get back up again, then that's great.

Resilience, at least in purely material terms, is the ability of something to return to its original shape when stretched. It's a mark of consistency that persists no matter what life throws at it, and this is exactly what founders need. You need to think about the kinds of things that will break your business. You also need to accept that there could be a 'black swan' event that you just can't foresee, and the only influence you can have is how you respond.[12] Competition slashing its prices and stealing your customers, your best staff being poached, a change in public tastes, that sort of thing. And from a personal point of view you need to think about the kinds of things that will break you: loneliness, criticism, lack of time, lack of money.

An early sign of founders who don't have this resilience is that they already have excuses lined up for every hiccup. They can't do anything until they have a technical co-founder. They can't move forward until they have investment. They can't make the time while they still have a full-time job. All of which, as proven by countless others, are complete rubbish.

In both cases, for you as an individual and for your business, the key is to develop genuine resilience by preparing yourself in practical ways for the stuff that the startup life will throw at you, by preparing yourself to keep your original shape, no matter how far you're stretched. That's what this chapter is about.

Keep on keeping on

We've noted already that if you're not willing to write 1,000 emails to potential customers, then you're in the wrong game. For one, if you can carve out the time and the energy to write those 1,000 emails and still rebound to your positive, vibrant self, then you're doing well. But more importantly, the very process of contacting 1,000 people – each of whom might well tell you to stick your stupid email – will help you develop the thick skin you'll need to survive building a startup.

---

[12] N. N. Taleb, *The black swan: The impact of the highly improbable* (2010).

If you're to be truly resilient – to take everything life throws at you and absorb it or deflect it without losing your shape – then you need to stay fit and healthy in both body and mind. To build resilience we need to practise self-care and recognize that it's not just okay but vitally important to maintain a strong inner core (literally and figuratively). This means getting enough exercise, eating right, treating yourself from time to time, spending time with loved ones or even on your own. It's important to understand that you don't need to be constantly 'on it'. Indeed, if you try to be, you'll certainly fail along the way when you burn out.

Another element of resilience is in how you deal with setbacks. It's okay to be sad about something going wrong or to have feelings of anger or frustration when dealing with the complicated and hard-to-control realities of building a business, but you need to be disciplined about how you deal with these scenarios. Allow yourself to process the emotions, take note of anything you've learned and then move on. How you bounce back counts, and by being disciplined in your approach to setbacks you will improve your resilience. It's very much a virtuous circle.

Resilience is a muscle you can develop, and, just like biceps or quads, the muscle needs to be put under stress over and over to strengthen and grow. By facing up to tough experiences and working through them methodically you will better prepare yourself for any problems that lie ahead. For this reason alone it's a good idea to face every tiny issue head on and to learn something about your business, and yourself, from that adversity.

It's not just us spotting this; it's a keen part of most investor observations too. Investors like to build ongoing relationships with the founders they will eventually invest in, and sometimes that can take a long time. This can of course be very frustrating when you're putting in time with an investor and keen to get some capital to drive forward your vision, but there's logic behind it. The investor wants to be sure that you do what you say you will, and that you do what you say you will even when things get tough. They want to see your resilience in action. They want to see that you'll continually show up. After all, actions always speak louder than words.

The good news, of course, is that, once they're convinced you're the real deal, they'll be much happier to trust their investment with you and back off.

Putting yourself out there

The most likely reason you'll fail at something is you. It's a hard but simple truth. It won't be the state of the market, or the people around you, or the product… it'll be you. First and foremost this is because you control all those other things, or at least your relationship with them. It's also because, ultimately, you only truly fail when you choose to stop moving towards your vision altogether. Only you can make that decision. Those who don't make that decision? They are the truly resilient.

There are lots of people with genuinely good intentions and good ideas who are simply not willing to pay the price for the success they thought they wanted: they don't bounce back from the inevitable setbacks; they blame others and have excuses when they could have pushed through. This doesn't make them bad people and it's no judgement of them as human beings, but it does mean they aren't cut out to build a business from scratch. It's why you need a strong personal vision, a real mission to drive towards and the resilience and discipline to get there. Indeed, you'll need everything you can get to drag you across the line.

If you're building a startup, then you'll be no stranger to the pitch deck. It's this document, more than almost anything else we've observed with founders, that gives a real idea of those who will keep going and those who will crumble. You see, a pitch deck might have to be re-written 100 times for 100 different conversations, and the reaction to having to do that is very telling.

For some, it's a bind, something to be avoided if at all possible and not really part of the process of building a business. For others, it's a golden opportunity, a chance to learn, evolve and improve everything they're working towards. Guess which founders find themselves with more successful businesses in the long run?

What's interesting about this in particular is that it showcases resilience as a really energizing trait. A task that many see as repetitive and grinding will be viewed by those with resilience as something to generate momentum. They can literally bounce themselves off these moments and springboard towards success. We see similar responses from founders at 9others dinners in how they accept and respond to input from others in the group.

Presenting your work to people also helps you deal with – and develop responses to – negative comments and disappointment as a kind of second nature. This is critical in ensuring that the negativity that comes along – and it will – doesn't derail you. You don't need to take online reviews personally or negative coverage in the press to heart. What you need to do is see these things for what they are – either helpful criticism or pointless negativity – and use them to spur you forward. Take the feedback, understand it and use it to help you improve. Resilient people don't avoid doing things in case someone on the internet says something nasty one day. If you're throwing in the towel because of that, then it's not the imagined naysayers who are stopping you – it's you!

The good news is that you can engineer all of this.

While most of us avoid conflict as a rule, we ultimately know that difficult conversations, setbacks, rejection and hard-to-handle people are inevitable. So why not lean into them? To engineer a more resilient persona, you simply engage with the tough stuff more often than you avoid it. As such, it's a question of asking yourself whether you'd like to develop your resilience to these things in your own time, under your own control, or if you'd like to develop it in a rush further down the line and when the stakes might be much, much higher. It doesn't seem terribly complicated when put like that.

There are other practical benefits to all this too. As a founder, regular exposure to the bad things (as well as the good things) in life will help you with your decision-making. When faced with new situations unfolding, you can recognize whether they will be good for your business or not, and therefore what steps you should take to either capitalize or mitigate. Of course, even if you get these choices wrong (which you likely will at some point), your resilience will help you draw everything you can from the experience while you bounce back into shape.

By seeking out – or even just not running away from – situations that will force you to trust your own resilience, you will improve your ability to bounce back and take stock of what really matters to you and your business.

The price of resilience

There are plenty of stories of founders who have gone through challenging times and come out the other side better for it. They're the stories we hear at almost every 9others dinner. There are the co-founder conflicts, where there was always a bit of resentment, mistrust and blame; the disappearing investors who only did the due diligence to get intel on a competitor of their portfolio; and the David versus Goliath legal challenges of trying to get invoices paid after clients reneged on a signed agreement.

They're important to hear because they do happen, and they might happen to you. Indeed, part of the 9others essence has always been to encourage these stories, which can easily be glossed over when founders are trying to impress each other (the small numbers and the Chatham House Rule[13] help this, of course).

There is a 'but', however. By being resilient you need to consider what you're choosing not to do. Everything, including resilience, has a price.

It might be that your increased resilience pulls you further away from your peer group and the world you initially inhabited. Not having excuses and not bowing to peer pressure can have the real effect of not fitting in anymore, which can be tough in itself. It can bring a real sense of guilt if you're 'moving on'

---

[13] The rule reads as follows: 'When a meeting, or part thereof, is held under the Chatham House Rule, participants are free to use the information received, but neither the identity nor the affiliation of the speaker(s), nor that of any other participant, may be revealed.' More on the other 'Golden Rules' of 9others in Question 5, 'What does it take to succeed?'

from the place and the people who have been with you for years. Or it could be that in developing resilience you're more inclined to take risks and move past a comfortable career with all the trimmings of a pension, bonuses and progression. This is hard too, especially if you have a family relying on you.

Investor Chris Sacca prefers investing in people who've done their time in 'crappy jobs' or travelled and worked in foreign cultures, for example. He's drawn to people who've had to ask for help or had to scrap to make their way. Hearing stories about people's lives gives us all insights into how they overcame the biggest challenges and what set them up to be so resilient. Where they grew up, what they did for money as a teenager, who they feel taught them the most about life, what they found really hard growing up. It's often these challenges in the first part of life that help develop a deep streak of resilience. As above, it also shows through the choices they've made: to move away, to change careers, to try something surprising. Those who demonstrate this, who have overcome challenges already, are always going to be more likely to succeed at what they do next.

The irony is that resilience is a less talked about attribute, chiefly because it's so obviously needed. People know that a founder's journey will be very hard, so it's laughed off as a given. This means it can be hard to understand the point we're making here: you need to prepare yourself for a tough journey ahead. This is not doom-mongering; it's common sense. Just as you need to work out how to pay the bills, you also need to work out how you're going to stay standing as you're battered by startup life.

From the dinner table

I had an early vision for creating a positive impact on people's lives and I have the ability to find doors in places where others only see walls. I was born in a refugee camp and lived there until I was 12, when I moved to Hebron, a city on Palestine's West Bank. Having lived most of my adult life in a conflict zone, I wanted to leverage entrepreneurship and my technical background to have a bigger impact on the world. I instinctively knew that opportunities could be afforded by remote working and, having benefited from that myself, launched MENA Alliances, which connects talented professionals in Palestine, the Middle East and North Africa with businesses all around the world. It's been a tough journey, but I'm glad I stuck with it as I'm incredibly proud of the thousands of graduates we've trained and the hundreds of jobs we've created.

– Abeer Abu Ghaith, founder and CEO of MENAAlliances.com

When I think about being resilient, I don't see it as getting beaten down then getting back up again, it's just how it is, and there's never a day that's 'normal' or chilled.

It might sound odd, but I sort of fell into the hospitality sector. I didn't set out and think, 'I want to do something in hospitality'. My career before this was as a social worker, and I was always interested in community and thought that a 'community space' could be done better and have a great impact. I'm now four years in and have built this strange beast of a business that's sort of in my image but also quite foreign to me. Kindred has a life of its own. We throw amazing art and music events, people meet and collaborate by working here, and I sometimes wonder how all of this started!

It has been a tough first few years, though. We opened in 2019 after I saw that there was a craving for this kind of physical space to meet, work and have fun. Then, of course, Covid happened – I could kind of see it coming and remember telling the team that this is probably going to be really bad; I didn't really know what we were going to do. I don't think I'm a natural or typical CEO – I've never wanted a hierarchy – so I was very open with the team about my own fears and vulnerabilities. I've realized that some people like working with someone like that and some don't. I know it can be confusing and unsettling, but I felt like I owed it to the team to be really open and honest, especially back in the early days.

I think that openness has helped me – and also the team – be resilient to the challenges that are thrown at us. I actually closed Kindred a few weeks before the first official Covid lockdown because I could see it coming and people were getting really wary. Again, I was open with the team that I might not be able to pay them – this was well before any of the government support was announced – and that was a really tough conversation to have.

However, as well as being an open and honest CEO I'm also a very optimistic one. During lockdown I took the opportunity to reset, to think again (even though we were a young business) about how we were doing things, and I was always optimistic that we'd be able to reopen at some point!

That optimism got me through the pandemic challenges and a lot of other challenges too. I do recognize the amazing and even privileged upbringing I've had – the support of parents and being told 'You can do anything!' from a young age is something not everyone has. I was always encouraged to try things and told it's okay if they fail and I learn from them. In particular, my mum was pretty hands off, so I was very independent and always thought, 'Sure, we can do it!'

Now I'm a few years into Kindred and I think I'm a different kind of leader. I've recently completed a masters at LSE and learned a lot more about myself and leadership, so I'm a bit kinder to myself and realize that, as I've been doing this since 2019, I don't need the reassurance of the team as much, so I'm less open with them about the challenges I have. In the beginning I was maybe looking for an external 'expert' too much, but I think I've made enough mistakes and had enough difficult conversations to realize that, more often than not, the expert is me!

I think all these experiences have helped me to keep going. I have to keep asking myself and others what's right for the community, but I also know I'll never be 'done'. Some entrepreneurs are striving to reach the summit, but I think of it as a longer journey across rolling hills. There's always another one to climb in the distance, so I have to enjoy the journey.

Entrepreneurs should be aware that they're signing up for a life that has lots of extremes and ups and downs, and I think we, the entrepreneurs, should just be excited about where we can take our lives and the impact that's possible.

– Anna Anderson, founder and CEO of Kindred London

Conclusion

Being a founder isn't an easy job, but it's one that offers you ultimate control. You need to make the most of that.

You will get knocked down, but you can always get up again. How quickly and easily you rebound is down to your experience and your understanding of what's happening, and that comes from consciously working to set the right conditions around you to develop your resilience. Just showing up each day is a strong start. Taking the tougher path as a matter of principle is good too. But you should also read and educate yourself widely, engage with others and learn their stories, keep yourself fit and healthy, and schedule in self-care when you don't actually need it yet. All of that will really help.

Practise the hard stuff when you have the time and energy to take something from it; don't wait until it smacks you in the face.

Questions to ask of yourself and others

What is the worst thing that could possibly happen to my business? What would I do to fix it? How do I currently recover from a setback? How can I make myself bounce back more quickly?

Each day, reflect on the difficult things and ask yourself: what have I learned today? What can I do differently next time? How can I be 1% better? How can I be 100% better?

In addition, you could try Peter Thiel's 'steel man argument' (see the questions at the end of Question 3 for more info) to think of the strongest arguments you can make against yourself. Be really tough, then try to see how you can develop and better cope with those arguments.

Finally, a question for others. Whenever you interact with someone, but especially when things have gone badly, ask for feedback. Ask: 'How do you think I'm doing?' Ask how the other person felt you could do better. Use every experience as an opportunity to learn and grow.

Question 5
What does it take to succeed?

We learned that if the day started well, it generally went well… And the discipline to get going early has always given us an amazing head start.

– Dan Land, co-founder of Coco di Mama

Question time: are you disciplined?

Andreessen Horowitz, an American venture capital (VC) firm, talks about certain founders as people always on the lookout for 'silver bullets' – the kind of magic, undiscovered, simple thing that will solve a problem in a flash. That's understandable. These founders are usually smart people who recognize that there may well be better solutions to the challenges we face in this world. And sometimes, these founders are even right. But (and this is the important bit) not often. What's much more likely, they believe, is the discovery of 'lead bullets'. Lead bullets are driven with sheer discipline deep into their target, and, unlike the mythical silver bullet, you might need a lot of them. A lead bullet gets its energy from staying a little bit later each night to get through a tough time – and inspiring the team to do the same. A lead bullet forms from using time and energy smartly to launch a feature quicker than the competition. A lead bullet turns up day after day after day, making a bigger and bigger dent each time. It can be a perfect bullseye hit, sure, but it's powered by relentless grunt work, not skill.

So the question is: are you disciplined enough to hit the target with a lead bullet? Or are you desperately hoping you've found a silver bullet that will do all the work for you?

Doing the grunt work

Alex Depledge was a co-founder of Hassle, a startup acquired for a healthy eight-figure sum in 2015. Hassle's business idea was a simple one: connect vetted cleaners with customers. Alex understood half of this equation, as she'd used a cleaner at home, but she didn't know what it meant to be a cleaner. This meant she had to do something she had not done before, something low waged that she, or others, may have snobbily seen as beneath her. But she had the vision and the discipline to do it.

This difficult step allowed her to really learn what the business needed. Did she commission surveys or do research? No, it was something that she knew she really had to get to grips with. So she did. There's no substitute for getting your hands dirty (in this case literally).

Alex had to put up with bad treatment and offers of cash-in-hand deals against agreed contracts while still leaving customers happy with the cleaning job at the end of a visit. While doing this, Alex also had to maintain enough of a distance to think as the founder of a tech startup looking to shake up the space. Doing all this helped clarify one very important thing: the service they were building as Hassle was really for the cleaners, not the clients. The real commitment to her work also helped Alex show she was serious, so access to millions in funding from top VCs – and a handsome exit in the end – became attainable too. In this case, discipline really helped Alex succeed. It helped strengthen the purpose behind her vision, and it built her resilience too. It really does pay to just get on and do it.

When we were starting 9others we would regularly meet for coffee at 7 am in Coco di Mama on Fleet Street. It was about halfway between our respective offices and it opened early (it was opposite Goldman Sachs after all). Dan, the owner, would often let us in at 6.50 am while he warmed up the coffee machine. It always surprised us that there weren't more coffee shops open at 7 am, and we definitely couldn't find any others that would let us in early on a cold morning (we tried, and never returned to, many!). We'll come back to Dan and his story shortly, but his kindness, energy and enthusiasm in that 90 minutes before work would always set us up brilliantly for the day. Turning up day after day for years on end on wet, windy mornings in the winter also made us realize that 9others is exactly what we want to do. We could have made excuses, not bothered to set the alarm clock or tried to fit things in around lunch or after work, but those excuses would have been the first nails in the 9others coffin. Instead, those early starts got us to our ten-year anniversary and beyond.

The discipline had knock-on effects for us both. To make this work, and make it easy, Katie would lay out all her clothes for the entire week ahead on Sunday evening. That way, she had one less thing to think about and could just get up, get sorted and get out the door each day. For Matthew, he sought inspiration from Barack Obama and others and started to wear the same thing each day – white shirt, jeans, jumper. They're small things, but the effects can really ripple through your life.

Your own flavour of discipline

When we work with founders, we're not looking for any particular kind of discipline. They just need to show discipline in *something*. A daily diligence or regular attention to something that matters to them and that shows their ability to practise and train their discipline muscle.

One way of seeing if a person has discipline is to see if they have a routine that they keep to.

It might be as simple as getting up in the morning, having a run, making their bed, reading their emails over a coffee and only then starting on work for the day. Or it might be having a cold shower each morning followed by two hours of reading. It could be something entirely different. What matters is a routine and structure that works for them and that can be repeated over and over, week after week, to trigger the kind of focused attention that building a startup demands. It's something you see time and time again, and indeed something that founders will, in our experience, happily talk about – even eulogize about – if you ask them. We don't think we've ever met a successful founder without a disciplined regime in their regular schedule. It's that important.

One reason for this is the sheer number of opportunities that founders have to be distracted: quick interruptions, approaches from salespeople, suddenly urgent tasks, real life popping up in the form of family and friends. Having a disciplined approach that can create a structure is very helpful here. It almost shields you from these elements and helps you focus on what's important. Going further, a clear structure and the discipline to work within it helps you understand what you absolutely need to get done each day and what you are happy to compromise on.

You've probably heard that it's the things you say 'no' to that really matter, and we've found that to be the case. Part of being disciplined is understanding what demands your attention and what doesn't. It's the feeling that you don't have to fill your diary or always have something new on the go. It's understanding that being busy isn't the same as being successful.

Write some rules

A practical way to keep things disciplined is to have some rules that can be followed. This is very useful for other team members, of course, but it can also serve as a clear and quick reminder to you of what you should be saying 'no' to (and what you need to ensure happens).

We have specific rules for hosting meals with 9others. These are rules we have always adhered to and that hosts must sign up to if hosting on our behalf. It's these rules that set us apart from other networking dinners, and it's these rules that have built the network into something specific that people either buy into or they don't.

We've listed 9others' five 'Golden Rules' below for you to examine. This isn't to say that you should do or even consider them. It's just to show how it looks in reality for us. You will, of course, have your own perspective on things. It matters not what your rules are, only that you have some.

Rule 1: Pricing structure

Tickets increase in price as they sell, the trade-off being that those who buy first are committing early and don't know who else is coming. Those that book the last couple of slots pay a bit extra, but they also have full knowledge that it will be a full dinner. We've often felt under pressure to give a discount, but we never do – buying a ticket to a meal with 9others is the first step in contributing, and we want everyone to do that before, during and after. If someone wants a 'discount', then they need to get in early to the next dinner.

Rule 2: Meal design

We keep the group small, specifically to ten people, and that includes us. We've resisted the temptation[14] to squeeze a couple more in or to fill a room with people just to squeeze extra revenue (our summer and winter parties[15] aside, which are a different beast altogether). With just ten people around the table, each person gets a good amount of time to talk about their challenges, and everyone can comfortably respond. A more modest group also promotes a sensible end point; we never wanted 9others to be an endless boozy night. Keeping a tight structure with a finite time frame means those who have to leave at a sensible time can do so without worrying they're missing out. It makes everyone so much more relaxed.

---

[14] We partly called ourselves 9others to ensure we didn't stray – it's in the name!

[15] We get the community together twice a year in a big traditional networking event as part of developing more connections (and as an excuse to have a good night out).

Rule 3: Curation

Or rather, curation with the lightest of touches. We experimented early on with complete curation, i.e., bringing together ten people who would all connect and have something in common, but we realized very quickly that it was no more likely to spark interesting things than a more random group of well-qualified people. However, once we have a few sign-ups for a dinner we always look and see if the evening is shaping up as a good fit for anyone specific we've met. We'll then reach out to them directly to suggest they come along.

Rule 4: No hierarchy

Arguably the principal rule. 9others is not about turning up to hear someone; it's about turning up to be part of something. We've had people in the past offer to come and 'speak' at a dinner. Some of these people you've probably even heard of, but it didn't chime with our vision (some understood our misgivings and came to the dinners anyway). We want everyone around the table to feel a core part of the dinner. So whether it's a first-time founder or someone who's been round the blocks more than a few times, they're all welcome. In fact, they're not just welcome; they're the whole reason the dinners work. Different people with different experiences and perspectives are the key to unlocking great responses to the challenges laid down by each diner. After all, everyone has something to contribute, and everyone has something to learn.

Rule 5: Off the record

We adhere to the 'Chatham House Rule', i.e., people share whatever they're comfortable sharing in the room, and people are free to share points made in the discussion, but not to reveal who made any particular comment. Everyone explicitly agrees to this rule at a dinner, and it helps build trust in the room.

From the dinner table

> *At the beginning, 5 am starts were a necessity to simply get everything done. But as things progressed, the 5 am starts became a core part of our approach. We learned that if the day started well, it generally went well. And since most problems revealed themselves to us by 6 am, we could crack on with fixing what had gone wrong. It also set a tone for the business and what we expected of our senior people in terms of discipline and application. And as we grew further, the early starts kept providing benefits. It built solidarity with the team, who had to be in to open stores and get the days going – after all, we know it's tough being in at that time. So my co-founder and I would each show up at a different store at 5 am each and every day to catch up with the team informally and support the opening. Critically this was rarely about checking up on the team; it was giving hard-working people an opportunity to be seen working hard by their bosses, and we found people valued that. It can quickly get soul-destroying if you're the one in at 5 am every day, taking pride in your opening, but no one has ever seen it. And the discipline to get going early has always given us an amazing head start. Once you start crunching through your work at 5 am every day, you find that, by the time most other people are in, you have done almost everything you need to do. It's a great feeling, getting on the phone with people at 9 am, feeling like you've done all your work for the day.*
>
> – Dan Land, co-founder of Coco di Mama

> *I've always strongly believed that people do business with people, not companies.*

After being in business for a while I had the inevitable negative experiences with clients, so I started to think if I could figure out a way to only work with people that I'd get on with and do great work with.

It was a bold step, but now I only work with people who've been referred to me through someone else I know and trust. This really tested me because it was incredibly tempting to react to interesting-looking inbound requests.

The thing is, though, just working with referrals shortcuts the 'selling' process. I'm not starting 'cold' and I don't have to try to convince people – I can just explain what I do and there's already a level of trust between us.

Funny thing is, referrals was actually a really negative thing for a long time running this business. I spent many years worrying about only being able to find new clients through referrals, and trying (and failing) to have clients find us cold. This is what so many businesses spend countless time and energy on, but for me there was a realization (which comes with confidence) that it would be a total waste of energy. When referrals are your only acquisition strategy, it also means you have to deliver with the clients you have, as they're the people who will recommend you. A good bit of pressure.

It's also just marketing 101, classic scarcity tactics: people want what feels exclusive or what they can't have.

I do have checklists and frameworks in my mind. It's a bit more of a feel thing and mostly built around (i) could I see myself talking to these people a few times a week, or am I going to dread it? (ii) do I think the business they're working on has potential (you can't polish a turd!) and is the team legit (not that they've done it before but do they have integrity)? and (iii) are they full of startup bluster and

> *unrealistic expectations (happens a lot with founder CEOs!)? I'm not sure if I can spot a winning business every time, but I have got good at picking out people who are full of shit!*
>
> *Good people don't refer bad people. It's a really reliable channel. I've had to get good at having coffee – that's a skill to learn and get better at.*
>
> *Discipline is linked to this – I have to make a judgement on it. Those signals come from the people, and I have to be strict with myself and my team.*
>
> – John Graham, founder of JG Etc

Conclusion

Yes, it's important to have a great idea and be inspiring and have some luck on your side too, but it's sheer effort that's really going to make you and your business a success.

This is generated through discipline. Having routines and sticking to them is important, as are basic rules for what you will and won't do. All of which is literally going to get you doing more, of course, but it will also showcase to others (investors, customers, potential partners and employees) that you're deadly serious about your mission. As with resilience, discipline is something you're in control of.

Discipline is a super-strength that anyone can cultivate; you just have to keep turning up.

Questions to ask of yourself and others

Here are some useful questions to ask to test your own discipline.

What do I expect of myself on a daily basis? It doesn't need to be a lot (in fact, it shouldn't be), and it doesn't need to be impressive; it just needs to be honest. What are the things that you know you can do that will make each day resonate so you feel fulfilled?

What do I expect of others around me on a regular basis? It might be similar to the previous answer, or it might be very different. Thinking about this question and clearly articulating an answer will make it much easier to bring others with you and help avoid frustration.

What do I already do every day? What would I like to do every day? What would I like to stop doing? This triad of questions will really help you get to grips with the things that are actually taking up your time. Once you know that, you're in a position to make decisions about what goes, what stays and what gets shuffled about.

Question 6
How do I get comfortable being uncomfortable?

If you wait for perfection, you'll never get started.
– Hector Hughes, co-founder of Unplugged

New question: are you comfortable being uncomfortable?

Achieving success (however you define it) will expose you to some discomfort. It's uncomfortable to stay disciplined, for example. The entire practice of resilience, as outlined already, is an exercise in managing discomfort – when you openly engage with those who don't really like what you're doing – so that you can learn, improve and grow.

More importantly, however, we see discomfort – or at least 'not complete comfort' – as the default state of running a business. As founders, we each regularly kid ourselves that everything is so wonderfully arranged and neatly sorted that we have achieved true 'comfort'. Really, this is just a trick to help us sleep or switch off for the day, and there remain countless things we need to do and improve to keep our business ticking. And that's before we consider the many things we haven't even worked out we need to worry about yet. This is the uncomfortable state we're bound to be in, but it's the founder's reality. We can either let it overwhelm us, or we can bed in and accept our fate.

You're not perfect

We all want to be liked and approved of. It's as true for our businesses and ideas as it is for ourselves. We like the external validation of someone else telling us what we're doing is good. It shows that we're on the right path if people like what we're doing.

Or does it?

It's easy as a founder to fall in love with your own idea, but that's a dangerous trap, and it's not helpful when other people stoke the flames of desire you feel for your own solution. After all, solutions are flighty things, and they only work in certain contexts and for certain times. That's because the world, its people and everything that goes on around us – laws, technology, tastes, climate – has a habit of changing. The key, therefore, is to be in love not with your ideas, but with the problem you're solving and the mission you're pursuing (which, to rewind quickly, is why you need to know your 'why').

But even worse than people drawing you into a cul-de-sac to tell you how much they love your ideas is people who wax lyrical about said idea… but then they don't buy it. Whatever the reason for this – they're not the target audience, they don't have the funds right now, they have bought into another ecosystem, etc. – it's kryptonite to your ability to work out the right way to solve the problem you've identified. And while it's nice to be liked, it's even nicer to be handed cash for your products or services.

But what does any of this have to do with perfection? Well, the danger we face when we become too interested in people liking what we're doing is that we seek out more of it. Since not everyone will like what we do, we can easily convince ourselves that it's only because we haven't quite perfected the idea yet. It's an easy trap to fall into. The discomfort of people telling you they don't like the sound of what you're doing is hard to take, so we naturally avoid it. But thinking slightly better of ourselves, we resolve to make sure nobody else feels that the idea falls short. As such, we strive to iron out the imperfections. As outlined above, doing this with a view to making people like your idea isn't going to get you anywhere.

So you need to set out to learn more by doing.

Get out there

We hosted the first 9others meal in December 2011. Many we spoke to said this was an act of madness. December, famously, sees people busy with Christmas parties and other end-of-year necessities. There simply wouldn't be any interest in fitting in an extra, new event at short notice. This could have been an excuse not to do it. Indeed, we could have sat with a calendar trying to find the elusive 'perfect date' to launch a 9others that everyone would fall in love with.

We didn't, of course. Instead, we went ahead and did it in December with a few hot dogs and sandwiches on offer and a couple of bottles of beer for each attendee. We even footed the bill of £114 to make sure price wasn't a reason to put people off and to ensure we'd get some feedback on the idea. It went okay, but when it came to January we had another little wobble. People would be detoxing, we were told; nobody would be interested in going out in the post-Christmas slump. And we nearly listened to them.

We were more nervous about January than December simply because we had more on the line. Not only did people have to actually turn up, but we'd asked them to pay, too. We put tickets on Eventbrite in advance asking people to pay up front to cover the cost of the meal. As it happened, we learned a lesson about the set-up of the evenings straight away. Guests ordered a couple of extra bottles of wine and we didn't have the guts, or maybe the good sense, to tell them they couldn't. Even though people had paid, the extra wine cost us about the same as the December dinner! It worked okay. It wasn't perfect, but it wasn't a disaster. Most importantly, we learned things. For example, we learned that there's no point marketing an event with ambiguity surrounding it. Unless there's a date, time, venue and price listed, people have every excuse to wait to buy.

As a founder, it's not your job to make everything perfect before launch; that would be impossible. Instead, it's your job to focus on learning as much as possible about the market and how your product fits in order to inform what you do next. So you gather data, collect feedback and analyse what happens every step of the way. Then you improve. If things go wrong, that's okay. As long as you have a better understanding of what to do next time, that's a win. While you're not going to generate a checklist of everything you need to do to reach perfection, you will learn what you need to be better. And that's all you're ever trying to be.

Once you have this mindset – that it's your objective to learn, not to deliver perfection – you will be able to get over any criticism thrown your way. It's not 'people not liking you', it's suddenly 'fuel to help drive your business forward'. As such, you can never lose.

There is not a single product or service that was built ready to go from the day of launch and went into the world to great success. Whether it's a name change, an audience shift or something much larger, everything goes through stages of improvement to become a household name. Even something as simple as the wheel took a long time to perfect after it first came into use. Lighter materials, the addition of tyres, methods for attaching wheels to vehicles, etc. have all improved and continue to be improved, even in 2020s. Something more complex has even more that can be developed.

Most businesses you're familiar with started with something simple that they put into the world to help them learn. If it's a tech company, the early process might have been very manual until they learned more about what their customers wanted and felt comfortable investing in building fully automated systems. For physical products, the first versions are often hacked-together 'Frankenstein creations' made from borrowed parts and held together with sticky tape. As long as the offer is representative of the solution you're testing and can be put in front of the right audience, you'll learn something. People are very forgiving of the early versions of businesses if you can tell a compelling story about your mission and what you're trying to do.

Even if you're further down the line with a shinier-looking product, slicker website or more mature offer, it doesn't mean you stop learning. Airbnb launched three times with a proper 'grown up' product before it was really noticed. The irony, of course, is that until you're noticed, nobody notices. So if things don't work, you learn what you can and try again. Nobody is going to remember how awful you were last time when you're offering something better this time.

Excuses excuses

Related to all this is the most corrosive of founder habits: the excuse that you can't do X until you have Y. I can't go to that client until I have a website. I can't get funding until I have a chief technology officer (CTO). I can't get a CTO until I have funding. These things might be easier if you have all your ducks lined up neatly and a huge helping of luck, but there are other ways. Even launching a tech project as a simple 'paper prototype' (literally something made with pen and paper or, if you're feeling fancy, a hacked-together explanation of the technology in PowerPoint slides) allows you to start discovering value. It gives you something to put in front of people, to tell them your mission and ask, 'What do you think?' Once you discover that stuff, there will of course be technology to build to make it more efficient and help you scale, but you don't need to have all that to get people behind you. To get people interested, you just need to act.

If you're making excuses – and feeling reluctant – it's possibly because you're scared. Chances are this is because you're uncomfortable with the criticism you expect to receive from releasing something that isn't perfect. But remember that criticism isn't personal, and you need to embrace it. As Tim

Ferriss, author of the *4-Hour* self-help book series, says, 'A person's success in life can be measured by the number of uncomfortable conversations he or she is willing to have.'[16]

As touched on in Question 4, you can seek out uncomfortable situations to build resilience and make yourself more able to engage with these experiences. It's as simple as having uncomfortable conversations when they arise in your personal life or elsewhere rather than avoiding them. A tip is to practise the actual words you would use out loud so you get the feel of them in your mouth and actively experience saying them. By practising out loud, and not just in your head, you aren't saying them for the first time when you're feeling under pressure.

A lot of what we've covered in this chapter is unlearning the rules of formal education. At school you're looking for answers that are 100% right and aiming for the top grade each time. You wouldn't turn in an essay or leave an exam without your 'product' being as perfect as you could possibly make it. But this is not a good parallel for life as a founder (or maybe real life at all). Or to make another school comparison: you no longer need to know the right answer before you put your hand up. Instead, you've got to put your hand up to know if you have the right answer.

Non-scalable things

The practical way into this is to do 'non-scalable things' that really allow you to get close to the detail and find the value. It's tempting to get too far ahead when you're excited by the

[16] Tim Ferriss on Twitter, 26 January 2015. Available from: https://twitter.com/tferriss/status/559731737992130561

possibilities that might come up, but asking 'what will happen when we get to 1,000 users?' when you don't yet have ten isn't terribly helpful. The idea is to put something out there and really understand what aspect of what you're doing has value for the audience you're trying to help. If, for example, your value is in content, then you might not need a fully functioning app to get to the next stage. An email newsletter or even a printed flyer might do. That's how you can take a real step forward and then learn more.

It's all an incremental process. You start with what you can handle given the time and resources available to you, and you slowly grow, develop and evolve. The startups that succeed begin by serving one small group of people and then working out their next valuable move. It's true for niche businesses that service a delighted, core audience, but it's also true for Amazon (books) and Facebook (university campuses). Trying to build something like Amazon as it exists now before launch doesn't bear thinking about!

As a final word, this isn't to dismiss high standards. Your standards should still be high, and you should always try to do the best you possibly can. But this is relative to your size, what you're creating and how you're presenting it. If you're showing a paper prototype of an app, then of course it will be simple, but it needn't also be ugly and carelessly put together. Similarly, it's very easy to build a nice-looking website now, but the same wasn't true in 2002, so people's expectations are different. So your presentation standards are necessarily allowed to be a bit lower. It has to be the best you can achieve with what's available.

From the dinner table

We wasted a lot of time on perfect. We spent a good six to eight months tweaking our first cabin. Some major things needed sorting – broken doors and emergency DIY. But we also got caught up in too many details. The details are important, but there's always an opportunity cost. We focused on that rather than growth. Then one day a friendly investor kindly ripped into us and one phrase stood out: 'Perfect is the enemy of growth.' You accept the imperfections with any startup. That doesn't mean you shouldn't focus on an amazing product; you should. But if you wait for perfection, you'll never get started. Ironically, it's the growth that allows you to attract the people and resources to take you to the next level. Get moving now, and worry about perfection later.

– Hector Hughes, co-founder of Unplugged

I got into the startup world 15 years ago after working in the music industry, and I joined an early stage, fast-growing startup as COO. The cliches are true – it was a baptism of fire, things were chaotic, lots of imperfections, and it was high risk. Over the next nine years I had three different non-founder but very early COO roles at high- growth startups. I'm a natural ops person – I like structure and processes, and I realize now that I was fairly unforgiving. I don't think I ever really got comfortable with being uncomfortable, but I knew that the imperfections and discomfort were the reality and probably wouldn't change.

Now that I'm a founder-CEO of my own company I'm more forgiving of those CEOs I worked for. The CEO role is so broad that you just don't have the luxury of striving for perfection. In becoming the CEO of my own startup I needed to release myself from the shackles of perfection and being involved in the details. And really, there's actually not a trade-off in quality of outcomes – the processes and things I do as CEO are different, but the vision and outcomes can be similar.

Could I have achieved more as COO if I hadn't gone into the details as much? I'll never truly know, and, on reflection, a lot of this comes down to confidence and experience, but I see now that a COO needn't try to boil the ocean. My co-founder now is an engineer, and we're good at pulling each other up when we go into too much detail. We say, 'Hang on, is this "small, medium or large"?' This rough categorization helps us know how much we need to think about it, otherwise we'd spend hours on the small stuff, when as CEO it's more important to make the decision quickly and document it for later.

There are three tactical and practical things that really help me now to be comfortable with being uncomfortable. First, at Boundless we write everything down, order our thoughts and do scenario analysis. I know I need to make a decision, so I look at all the ways it could go and how it could impact our customers. It turns out it's often the scenario you discount at the beginning as 'obviously' being wrong that is actually the right, but often hard, thing to do.

Second, Tim Ferriss talks about 'fear setting'. It's like goal setting, but with your fears. You have to think: what is it I'm worried about? You write down all your worst fears and the impact of each happening, plus what you can do to mitigate them and, should the worst happen, how bad they would actually be.

Finally, 'rubber ducking' – everyone in my team has a rubber duck on their desk that they talk to. It sounds crazy, but we talk to our rubber ducks and tell them a problem we're facing. It has to be said out loud, and the point of it being a rubber duck is that the team doesn't expect an answer in return. It's purely that the process of addressing a problem out loud can then unlock a solution or make you realize it's not actually a big problem after all.

I believe that, subconsciously, we often think about the bad outcomes so much that they feel really big in our own minds, and we need to talk them through with someone we trust. Discomfort might actually be the way to go, so while you're in this startup game you have to get comfortable with it.

– Dee Coakley, co-founder and CEO of Boundless

Conclusion

It's easy to get caught up in your own idea, and it's easy to get swept up in the adoration of people who like this idea, but neither of these things is helpful. Instead, you need to accept the reality that your idea isn't perfect and not everyone is going to like it. When you do, you'll start to better understand what you need to do to actually grow your business.

'Doing stuff' is what it's really all about. 'Perfect is the enemy of good', as they say, and indeed, as Hector notes above, 'the enemy of growth'. Trying to achieve perfection simply delays you in getting out there to talk to people, test your solutions and make deals or build your team. So by all means build something decent, but know that the time to get out there and start showing off your work is probably much, much sooner than you think.

There's no such thing as perfect; trying to achieve it is a waste of energy you could put into doing something that simply works.

Questions to ask of yourself and others

What's stopping me? Or, to put it another way, what's your greatest fear about just making things happen? Sometimes, 'striving for perfection' is really a cover for something else, an excuse to not get out there and start doing stuff. Be honest with yourself.

What's the worst thing that could happen? Or what's the worst someone could say to you or write online? And what would happen if they did that? How would you respond? How would it change your approach or your business? If you wouldn't change anything, then stop worrying. If you would, then change it before anyone notices.

What hypothesis am I trying to test? Of course, it's important to do your research and get things in order before pushing forward, but you need to be clear. You might also ask yourself what you need to gather data on, for example (but make sure it's an actual NEED and not just a way to avoid doing the hard stuff like getting out and selling!).

How can I go from zero (nothing) to one (something)? Once you're at one, it's easier to move on to two, three, four… but the zero-to-one step is the hardest. So work out how you can find the energy and impetus to get going and make that leap.

Question 7 What does success look like?

I'd define success for me... as something like being able to live the life that I've chosen/designed in that moment with the limitations that I have taken into account.

– Alex Somervell, co-founder of One Third Stories

At the end of the day, the goal is, by your own definition, to achieve 'success'. To be happy and proud of what you've achieved, and to maybe even achieve *more* than you ever expected; what Richard Koch has called 'unreasonable success'.[17] It might be counted in cash, or memories, or connections, or knowledge gained, or awards won. It doesn't matter. Just remember to define it and, when it comes along (even the seemingly small successes along the way), embrace it and celebrate.

---

17 R. Koch, *Unreasonable success and how to achieve it: Unlocking the nine secrets of people who changed the world* (2020).

Every founder needs to remember that their ultimate goal is to drink in that success.

Recognizing success

We need to know what success looks like so we can recognize it when it comes along. It's so easy as a founder to get so caught up in the day-to-day activity of growing a business and servicing your customers that when success, as you've defined it, comes along to say hello, you don't even notice – let alone celebrate.

It's so crucial that you do celebrate, though. When you're on such a challenging journey you need to punctuate it with moments of positivity and take the chance to enjoy what you've achieved. And that should extend – with relative merit, of course – to both the bigger wins and the tiny ones.

One simple way to think about success, if it's not already clear to you, is to think about failure and what that would look like for you. Not being able to work in this business in one year? Ten years? Being publicly shamed or embarrassed? Finding yourself back as an employee in a nine-to-five job? Another way still is to imagine your business in its most successful form in your eyes. Is that selling it for £1 million? Or it being bought by a certain behemoth? Is it an initial public offering (IPO) north of £1 billion? Is it to die while still running the business you've built? Or to hand it on to your kids? Again, it doesn't matter what the answer is, but it can really help to crystallize what it is you're working towards.

As you'll have noticed already, this isn't just about money.[18] Money is easy to quantify and track, so it's a reasonable place to start. But we've noticed that, just as money is easy to quantify, it's easy to challenge. Say a company sells for £100 million. Why didn't it make £101 million? Why didn't it sell much earlier for £50 million and save a lot of time and heartache? It's basically easy to knock large sums of cash, and this can leave founders unsure if they were really successful. Yes there's lots of money in their bank account now, but is that really what they wanted? After all, it's just a number. Our observation is that it's much healthier, and indeed more pragmatic, to find some other form of success that you're reaching towards. A non-monetary measure (e.g., building a company that survives a certain amount of time, or employing a certain percentage of the local community) is harder for people to challenge you on directly, doesn't fluctuate as much over time (a successful exit when you start may have a zero added, or taken off depending on the economy, by the time you're ready and able to sell) and sets you apart from a direct comparison with other companies where money is, as it were, direct currency. Ultimately, having your own story of success builds an inner confidence that cannot be faked; it helps drive the mission you're on.

---

[18] It's not that having money as your goal is a bad thing, of course. In fact, it can be a very impactful goal with many founders going on to recycle it back into the startup ecosystem. This is something that's changed in the time we've been running 9others. Back in 2011, on the whole, people made money then disappeared to their country house or boat. Now exited founders are angel investors, LPs in funds and trusted advisors to founders taking the first steps on their journey.

Staying focused

The time taken to work out what success looks like isn't just valuable for you as a founder; it will also resonate further within the business. Just as drinking in new ideas from social media, networking events or our reading list can both shake our confidence in what we're doing and encourage us to pursue paths that might not be right for our own businesses, the same can happen to your staff. But if there's a very clearly defined measure of success that's constantly referred to and held up as the destination everyone is working towards, then it is much, much easier for everyone to stay the course.

We often come across entrepreneurs who don't actually know why they're building a business, and this feels like an awful lot of work and risk to us. The rise of technology, or maybe the access to tools that make it easy to deploy a tech business, has seen companies raise huge amounts of money, scale very fast and then exit at speed. WeWork is perhaps a good example of this. The shared-office-space company raised over $20 billion from venture capitalists and was privately valued at almost $50 billion. WeWork did exit, but for around $10 billion, and since that IPO, the share price has dropped by 80%. Was WeWork overvalued? Should a business like that have taken venture capital? Was it a 'tech startup' or actually a typical real estate business? The headlines around these kinds of businesses and their necessary 'fame' have easily led others to see this glorified vision as the only way to build a business. The irony, however, is that raising investment is not a business model. And while, for some, that huge scale, VC-fuelled approach is the right way to go and the business being built just couldn't succeed without it, for many (or most) others, it's not right at all.

For one, when you need lots and lots of money to make things happen, the main job of the founder is to fundraise. While some founders thrive on that, many don't. Others think they can fundraise first then just get on with the work, but it probably won't work out like that. The founder will be raising, raising, raising while others execute and build the company. And, of course, if there's no eventual exit for a founder and everything dies away, then what was it all for? If you love fundraising, then maybe it's okay. But if you're trying to do anything else, you might want to consider another path.

Stefano Marrone once shared with us the illustrative story of a tennis champion who wins Wimbledon. What people see is someone who must have had a huge desire to win a Grand Slam. Someone for whom winning is a driver. But the reality is that the greatest champions ultimately love playing tennis and improving their game. They love the conditioning, the tactics, the practice matches, the training sessions themselves. They might find them boring and difficult at times, but that's just being human. At the heart of it all, playing tennis and getting better is what they do, *that's* what they're all about. Winning Wimbledon is just an outcome of that. To win Wimbledon, you really need to love the practice. The same is true for film-makers: to produce great movies you better really love being in the editing room cutting frame by frame, not just kicking back with some popcorn watching the end result on the big screen or collecting the awards.

The point of all this is, of course, that there are various ways to build a business. MailChimp, a huge tech success story, didn't take VC money and bootstrapped its way to a $12 billion acquisition. That's definitely financial success (though whether it was success in the eyes of the founders, we don't know).

Most businesses, by volume at least, are good, solid lifestyle businesses: entities that generate enough income for the founder to have the lifestyle they want. This could be a little or a lot, but it certainly doesn't involve perpetual fundraising.

Define your success, not someone else's

There's a regular dichotomy that rears its head at 9others dinners – go big or go deep. One is the 'Uber model' – huge scale, cheap offer, for everyone. The other we call the 'Seth Godin model', named for the renowned marketing guru with whom Matthew spoke on stage (as mentioned in Question 2) who is very much a fan of this approach – narrow scale, hugely expensive offer, targeted at very few potential customers. Often, people will arrive at 9others with some traction in their business and be torn on which of these to pursue (albeit likely not at these extremes).

The problem arises when they try to do a bit of both, and knowing what success looks like would certainly help give them some direction.

In the early years of 9others we were aware of several 'networking' companies who had exited for decent money. As we've noted previously, this led us down some paths that involved conversations about funding, commercialization, data collection, business models and so on. It would have meant more people at more dinners.

But this wasn't what we did, or wanted to do. What we did do, and wanted to do, didn't fit this model of investment and exit. As such, we knew what we had to do to scale and exit, we even knew all the right people to make it happen, but we didn't do it. We knew that it wasn't what we wanted to spend our time and energy building. There was also, to be totally clear on this, the limitations we had on our time and our lack of desire to leave our day jobs, which made running just one dinner in London each month appealing in itself.

The two are related, of course. In the early days we wanted 9others to fit in with what we were already doing. This was part of the appeal. Over time, as we grew and expanded and it took more of our time and energy, we stuck to our principle of 'quality over quantity'. Doing so is what helped us build trusted relationships, and it's the compound interest we earned on these that has made the journey so valuable and created countless interesting opportunities elsewhere.

One of these was an idea we tested for scale in 2012. It was the second year of the Digital Shoreditch Festival, and we partnered with organizer Kam Star to run 20 dinners in a fortnight. For us, and for Digital Shoreditch, it was a huge success that helped get us into the hearts and minds (and stomachs) of a lot of new people. And it really made us think: what did scale look like for 9others? What was this element of our vision of success? Despite everything we believed and knew was working for us, maybe there was an appetite for people to come in large numbers to dinners that could be run concurrently.

But here's the thing. Although this opportunity was right there in front of us, something was missing – our enthusiasm. Making this change would require more work, more investment and more technology. All of which we could muster. If we wanted to. But we simply didn't.

What the experience taught us is that 9others isn't about running dinners, and certainly our success can't be measured by running more dinners or getting more people through the door. We want to connect people and solve the challenges they're each facing. We want to help them by being useful, and the dinners are simply the mechanism by which we do this. The buzz that we get from 9others, that drove us to meet at 7 am in Coco di Mama every week for years and that has driven us to write this book, comes from making these connections.

Dinners are, and will always be, a huge part of 9others.[19] For one, they're the thing people see; they're visible. But they also help us generate new connections and seek out support that takes us to new ideas. As we've outlined, it's the connections we're really excited about. One lesson we hope you'll take from this is that what you do and *how* you achieve your mission can be distinct things. Just as there's no right vision of success that suits everyone, there's no right way to achieve your success. It just has to work for you.

Yet despite being clear about what we were trying to achieve and working in a way that suited us, we still felt a slight niggle that we were missing something in terms of clearly defining success. So we took our own medicine and went to get the support of others to find some answers.

We had various conversations with people we knew would ask us hard questions. We also made sure to always have these conversations together, as a pair, so we could both stare into the headlights and be forced to face up to these questions without

[19] Matthew often says that, even if he hit the £€$ jackpot or everything goes wrong, he'll still stay grounded with one 9others meal a month.

the chance to sanitize our answers or second guess each other. We knew we might be making assumptions about what each of us wanted to do, and this seemed the quickest, most productive way to make sure we were moving in a direction that suited us both.

One person we spoke to was Mark Adams, a board advisor and marketing expert, who asked us the simple question: 'How do you want 9others to grow?' As often happens in these circumstances, it wasn't actually something we'd asked ourselves. We said that we wanted to see 9others all around the world. With entrepreneurs travelling and operating in a global market, 9others should be borderless. We all nodded. Then Mark asked, 'Okay, so how do you get started?' Katie blurted out that maybe we could do 12 cities in the next 12 months. New places to host 9others dinners. And, well, that became a plan.

With the right question, we were able to unlock a new version of success – to see 9others flourish around the world, making connections, via dinners, that were fruitful for all involved. It didn't matter that we didn't know which 12 cities, or how the logistics would work, or what responsibilities we would have versus local hosts. It mattered that this chimed with us and our mission. It was the right vision of success for us to try and attain over the coming year.[20]

So success for us is connecting people together.

It's also for 9others to still exist in another ten years' time.

---

20 We did it, by the way. First, we made a list of all the cities we thought 9others should be in – New York, San Francisco, Paris… – but it didn't turn out that way. We were in Papua New Guinea before San Francisco, and we've not yet hosted a meal with 9others in Paris. 9others took hold in the cities where the people needed it most.

And maybe, crucially, it's to still exist in 10 years' time with the exact same essence we had at the very first dinner.

A great example from our network is James Bishop. As a fledgling entrepreneur he had a faint, fuzzy idea of what he actually wanted to do, but a very clear idea of what success looked like for him. At that time, James found himself with the opportunity to run bars at the Glastonbury Festival and discovered that, if he managed things the right way, he could make enough money in that short stint to last out the rest of the year. This would, he contended, then allow him to spend time and energy exploring what else he wanted to do (because it wasn't to run bars at music festivals forever) and spot interesting trends and opportunities all around him. So his marker of success was 'to earn enough at Glastonbury to pay the bills for a year'. This took planning and preparation, but it was a clear goal. And while it was money based, and of course James had a figure in mind, the accumulation of cash wasn't the point. By doing this for a few years, James eventually worked out that his heart lay in podcasting, and he's now the founder of One Fine Play, a hub for podcast creators born from a successful production studio.

James ended up using his vision of success to spirit him towards a business he wanted to run. Of course, he now has new ideas of what success looks like for One Fine Play, and that's okay too. If we can recognize success, then, logically, we can also update our sense of it when we achieve things along the way.

All of which, you might have noticed, brings us neatly back to your mission and why you're doing what you're doing.

From the dinner table

I think it's really hard to articulate how important it is to really think about what you want and not sound patronizing or obvious. The reality is that very few of the ideal outcomes founders actually want are achieved via VC, if you think about it logically. Most people/founders want to do something they enjoy, earn good money and decide what to do with their time. I genuinely think VC is one of the worst ways to achieve those things! Though it can be an amazing way to achieve something if all you want is to make a mark in the world and you're willing to sacrifice life and short-/medium-term balance (and possibly happiness). I think I'd define success for me, therefore, as something like being able to live the life that I've chosen/designed in that moment with the limitations that I have taken into account.

– Alex Somervell, co-founder of One Third Stories

I think I knew this was definitely going to be for me as (i) I'd lived my life on a farm in a small village where nobody ever found my house, and (ii) I'd done a career for ten years (live music) where every day we showed up somewhere new and the 'address' we were given was never sufficient enough to find the loading entrance. In the music business, this was far further than the UK: we did the music for the F1 Grand Prix in Bahrain and travelled to remote villages in Ireland, mountaintops in Italy, remote countryside homes in Northern Nigeria and the back of stadiums in London. They all shared the same issue. I just felt like I was especially aware that there was an issue to be solved, and when we came up with the solution, I knew straight away I was going to make it my mission.

– Chris Sheldrick, co-founder of what3words

Conclusion

If you don't know where you're heading, you won't know when you get there. It's really important that you take time to examine what success means to you and do so without worrying about what society, or your peers, might think. Your success is personal, and that's critical.

It might come quickly, it might take some time, and your vision of success might change along the way. That's all okay. It's your choice and your prerogative. Get help if you need it, and take a step back if you need it, too. Just always know what your destination is so you can enjoy it when you arrive.

You create your own business to achieve what you want to achieve, so make sure that remains the focus, no matter where things take you.

Questions to ask of yourself and others

Why am I building this business? You should be able to go back to your 'why' (see Question 1) to help with this, but it's good to look at it specifically within the context of striving for success.

What does success look like for me? You might want to think about things like the kind of income you're hoping for or how much time and control you want over your life. Or maybe you measure success in another way. Whatever it is, in order to measure it and recognize when you achieve it, you need a target to aim for. Consider things such as money, lifestyle, location, how the business will be funded, how many employees you want to have, how big the business can or should be, how your role might change over time and anything else that strikes you as important.

Question 8
Who can help?

I have always regarded entertaining as a vital and underrated part of business – especially when times are tough. After all, forging and building relationships is really what business is all about. And there's no better way to take a relationship to the next level than a good meal in the right setting.[21]

– Roland Rudd global chairman of FGS Global

Business is about people. However you do it, whatever your business, you're ultimately dealing with people. And your success (however you define it, see Question 7) is therefore going to be a result of the people you connect with and the dealings you have with them.

---

[21] This quote from Roland Rudd did a great deal to validate our thinking before we launched, so much so that it appears on links to all 9others events. J. Stimpfig, 'Roland Rudd's dining boltholes', *Financial Times* (12 June 2009). Available from: https://web.archive.org/web/20140828172741/http://howtospendit.ft.com/food/34-roland-rudds-dining-boltholes

An active and engaged network *of people* is key to your success. But a network can't just be summoned out of nowhere; it's something that takes time, energy and enthusiasm to cultivate. It's also something that needs to be approached in a very purposeful way. The network you need when you're starting out, for example, differs from the network you need when you're trying to sell your company, even if there's overlap. However, key principles remain for building a network at all times and ensuring you have the right support around you when times are tough. Running a business can be very lonely, so it's best to surround yourself with people who can be there when you need them.

Moral support isn't the only benefit of a strong network, of course. The more people you know you can rely on, the more knowledge you can tap into and the better access you have to all sorts of things: insights, potential staff, last- minute room hire, recommendations for tools and services, nice dinner companions.

All of this is the pay-off for having a strong network, but you have to put the work in first.

Build it before you need it

The nice thing about a network is that, with the right effort, it grows naturally. You plant the seeds early, nurture the relationships and, over time, great things blossom. As such, you need to build your network before you can really harvest it. This should be obvious, of course. While it's very easy to help out an old friend, you're very unlikely to drop everything to help a total stranger who just dropped into your life minutes ago. The same probably goes for that person you spoke to once ten years ago and are only hearing from again now because you've moved into a new job or come into some money.

As we have always said at 9others, your success requires the aid of others – and that's what this is all about. You might not know who those others are or when you'll need them exactly, but you will certainly need most of them eventually. We think of it like a bank account, but instead of filling it with money, you fill it with goodwill. The goodwill that you generate over months and years can then be exchanged for favours and support when you need it. Everyone accepts goodwill to a greater or lesser extent, so as long as you have some in the bank, you have options.

The original format inspiration for 9others was a gentleman by the name of Roland Rudd. You will have read his quote at the beginning of this chapter. We were inspired by his ideas of bringing people together in loosely curated events as a way to seed trusted relationships and, in particular, of doing so over a meal, which is inherently social. We loved the concept of something that requires people to help each other out (passing things, pouring things) and to be together at a vulnerable time, i.e., when refuelling. These interactions build trust and unlock ideas, information, decisions and access far quicker than in many meetings. It's networking in a supercharged environment to start people on the important journey of making more connections, more regularly. Although, of course, it's what happens to these relationships after the bill has been settled that really matters. But more on that shortly.

Another aspect of building a network worth noting is what a good network even looks like. Do you need hundreds of contacts in your phone to make a real impact? Or is something more manageable worthwhile?

From our experience it's useful to have a 'core' network of people that you can keep going back to for support on a long-term basis. You may well have others with specialist interests who exist on the periphery of this group, but you need to find your own nine others who you can really nurture and provide your own support to in return, and who will have enough of a breadth of knowledge and experience to be a network that can offer real help.

You may be familiar with the power of having a great advisor, coach or mentor in your life, and it can be useful to think of a network as serving a similar purpose. Better than simply relying on one person to unlock all the wisdom of the universe for you (or every door to useful help and bountiful funding, for that matter!), you're building a balanced universe of individuals with different skills and specialities who can each be helpful in their own way.

Networking is hard

Like anything worthwhile, networking is hard. You have to get out there and put in the time, the miles and the conversations. You have to instigate, you have to follow up, you have to make the effort. And while you have to start now (there is no better time to start), the benefits of what you're doing might not come for months, or even years. But they will come.

So to make things a bit easier, the rest of this chapter is essentially going to be a practical rundown of the things we've learned over the years about building effective networks.

Let's start with the psychological barriers, of which there are basically two.

The first is the sheer weight of implication that drips from the term 'networking'. It conjures up images of shiny suits and business-card holders and quick, aggressive pitches machine-gunned at an audience chewing on canapés and unable to effectively respond. Or, at the very least, of incredibly dull conversations with people you're unsure about.

The second is what we might call the trading element. In order to grow an effective network that will help you, you have to help others. Sometimes you will find yourself thinking, 'What's the point?', especially when you're doing it for nothing tangible in the immediate term.

The thing with both snap judgements about networking is that they're based on a misunderstanding of what networking really is. Networking, quite simply, is *whatever activity is effective in building a network that is of value to you* and what you are trying to achieve. Part of that is being comfortable – nay, even enjoying! – doing it, and this means accepting that, if you want to be part of a network, you need to pull your weight too. Otherwise you're just surrounding yourself with people you expect to work for you for free, which is a bit weird – and not cool.

Networking can also be uncomfortable. Walking up to strangers at events or making a connection in another way is frightening. We get nervous and worry about all the things that could go wrong. Thing is, the person we're contacting or walking up to, cold canapé in hand, probably feels the same and would welcome hearing from a new, friendly face.

As you start and continue to build your network, you'll need to talk to people. This is just something that will happen, so try not to be shy about it; focus on the value you can give to others. If you go into conversations knowing that you have something interesting to share (which you should if you're remotely confident about what you're doing!), then it will be less 'Why would they want to speak to me?' and more 'I wonder where this conversation will take us?' It should be exciting to make new connections (even if they're just a passing point on the way to your next explosive meeting).

A good way to break the ice at events with speakers or panels is to start with something like, 'What did you think of…', 'I really enjoyed…', 'Do you know a lot about…', which you can toss to anyone in the room afterwards. Pure networking events don't offer this, so if you're uncomfortable in these spaces, then don't force yourself into them!

That said, you do need to be proactive. Find the events that will suit you, research conversation topics with people you want to connect with, put yourself in positions where you're having conversations with lots of people (a 9others dinner, dare we say, is the perfect antidote to even the most reticent networker, but there are plenty of other events that are just as welcoming and useful).

Something else that's useful to remember is that none of us are starting from scratch. Yes, some will have the privilege of family connections or university networks while others do not, but we've all got connections that can help us take a step forward. Family, friends, neighbours, former colleagues, schoolmates, local businesspeople in your area you might have interacted with (the local newsagent is an entrepreneur!), online connections… They're all someone to start with. Sure, you might be new to a particular city or scene, but you might already know someone who knows someone they can connect you to. Your newsagent might have a sister in the same field as you who's just moved to that town. You don't know if you don't ask – or rather, if you don't share with people what you're up to and who you're looking to connect with.

Another thing people stumble on is timelines.

On the one hand, many seem to think that they should know what transactional event should happen during the very first meeting – booking a coffee in, getting some specific information, making a specific introduction, making a sale – but this is unrealistic. Transactional stuff rarely happens straight away, and even when it does it doesn't mean you need to reciprocate in kind. A first meeting is just that, a chance to see if there's a connection you might explore further. If you think of it like dating, it might make more sense. You probably wouldn't propose marriage or a long weekend away on the first date.

It's true of the networks we want to build to help with funding, hiring, sales, advice and anything else. It can sometimes take years and years for conversations to become transactional, and that's okay; it's totally normal. The point is, don't leave it all until the last minute; you have to build your network long before you really need it.

Some more practical points

In our work of bringing people together and meeting people ourselves, there are some things that we know work. What sort of event should you go to? For a start, go to events you're genuinely interested in. That way, you'll have more genuine conversations with people afterwards. Don't go because you think you should; go because you know you need to.

If you go to the same or similar events enough times, then you'll get to see the same faces. It takes time for people to remember who you are, what you do and what you're like. These, however, are the people who are genuinely interested in building their own network too.

Find a diverse range of people and events. Be open and listen to people whose points of view don't match yours. That goes for everything, from age and background to the industry people are in, the role they hold and more.

It's not about having an ever-increasing number of people; it's more about tending to a crowd of people who will come and go.

Build a habit. This is not about attending one magical event where everything will be solved; it's about attending the right things regularly over many years and knowing that it will come good eventually.

Use your discipline. There are lots of reasons NOT to network, so you need to set yourself up so that you'll make the effort: go to events on the same day each week, pick locations that you can get to easily, pay for tickets in advance. Free events are great but easy to cancel – and remember others do too. If you sign up for paid events, then it hits you in the pocket if you don't go. Other people will also be thinking this, so such events are generally more productive.

Once you've been at a few of the same networking events, it can be a good idea to get to know the organizers. An easy way to do this is by offering to help – check people in, help with the tech/projectors, bring people along, recommend someone for a panel, etc.

If it feels uncomfortable, then invite a friend or colleague along.

Your network begins with you and one other person. If you know a couple of people but they don't know each other, then all three of you could go for coffee. That way, you're the connector. Then the 'rule' could be that, for the next coffee in a couple of weeks, you each have to bring one new person. Rinse and repeat. In a few short months you'll all have an amazing network of new people.

If you spot a 'connector', then make a special effort to get to know them. Some people just love to connect others and are naturally good at expanding their network. If you're on their radar it can help immensely (but remember to help them too!).

Get curious about others. Have a reason to talk to people that's not just about selling them something or promoting yourself or your company. You may need to practise this in advance, but that's what almost all the best, most natural-looking conversationalists do. Really.

Build your network before you really need it – cold-email people you admire, tell people you like them, aim high. Getting your name in front of people slowly builds familiarity. And don't be afraid to take the lead/ownership and set up a calendar invite and suggest locations; they can always be changed. Don't get stuck in a back and forth over logistics that will destroy anyone's enthusiasm.

At the end of it all, you're trying to build trusted relationships at a steady pace. By taking control of your networking (rather than floating around hoping to bump into others) you get to be part of the community you want and ought to be part of, and that will always be the most useful network for any of us.

From the dinner table

In Yemen we've targeted more than 500 entrepreneurs to help solve problems that entrepreneurs are facing in their businesses. People, especially women, have increasingly sought new sources of income by setting up small businesses that can help them be self-reliant. The promotion of networking activities had a very important role in addressing and discussing the challenges facing entrepreneurs and how to solve them by connecting to others.

– Yusra Hussin

The vision for ComplyAdvantage was to try and finally solve the problem of money laundering and terrorist financing. Many companies had tried and failed to build a system that could keep track of every person and company that would be a threat – whether through corruption, sanctions evasion or terrorist financing – but the potential of new technology made this possible for the first time.

I never wobbled on the solo founder part – I just knew this had to be done. If there was someone I felt would have been a huge value-add, then I would have had them join, but at that stage in time there was nobody in the frame, so I opted for 'no one' rather than 'anyone'.

– Charles Delingpole, founder and executive chairman of ComplyAdvantage

Conclusion

A network is something you cultivate slowly over time, not something you build with speed and aggression. Whoever you are, however you like to work and whatever you're doing, you can find a way to meet new people and offer them value. This is the basis of a network.

As long as you remember that it will take time and effort – and you're willing to invest both – then you'll be surprised by the opportunities your network surfaces for you.

It's always about people; after all, there isn't really anything else.

Questions to ask of yourself and others

Who do I already know who could help? And don't just think of professional connections. Family, friends, friends of friends, local businesses you shop in, school or university peers. Be open and ask around.

What gaps do I have in my network? If you can identify gaps, then you can make a plan to fill them. At which point, think about when you're going to tackle these gaps, where you'll find people and how you'll get into the right situations.

What value can I offer in return for those who help me? Whether it's a close friend or someone you've just met, you need to think about your end of the bargain. Why would they help you? What might tempt them to be even more helpful?

Where are the boundaries? Think about whether you have a demarcation between private life and business. Do they merge into one, or do you keep things separate? There's no right answer, but it's important that you have a clear sense of boundaries.

Are your connections all the same? Volunteer for things in your community to broaden your circle. Volunteering at charities or local trusts is not only good for the soul, it also helps diversify your network and therefore your ideas and insights.

Question 9
How do I keep the right people around me?

Maintaining a network is something that I've always seen as of paramount importance to my life and career, but probably not for the reasons you'd expect.

– Lauren Hine, chief of hub operations at AND Digital

We're nearly at the end, so here's an easy one: what happens when you stop looking after something?

Well, generally speaking, and sad as it is, it dies.[22] It's true for plants and rabbits, it's true for skills we have and it's true for your network. There's absolutely no point putting all the effort

[22] With a network, it'll be a slow, sometimes unnoticeable, death... until you need it. We've often said that, if we suddenly stopped hosting 9others dinners, nothing negative would happen immediately. But after a few weeks or a few months we'd notice that we weren't as insightful, useful or connected as we once were.

into building a network if you're not going to maintain it. The point of maintenance is to keep the network alive by making yourself memorable (even the most striking haircut can't manage that alone) and by always being in a position to seek, or indeed offer, help or other support.

That's not to say some people won't drop out of your network as their lives change direction or they find themselves on the other side of the world. This is natural, and it's okay, but it's all the more reason to make sure you're constantly working on your network, expanding it and looking after those you want to keep closest.

Know your tribe

A key aspect of getting your head around network maintenance is to understand your 'tribe'. This has two parts to it: who are you, and who do you serve. You should have a handle on who you are and what you want by now, but the question of who you serve is something worth spending more time on.

So who is it that you serve? Who are your tribe? Don't make the mistake of trying to make it everyone. You cannot be all things to all people. It's okay, therefore, to define yourself quite clearly as someone who is worth having in other people's networks for very particular reasons. This may be related to your expertise, or it may be that you're very connected in a particular geographic area or particularly good at spotting interesting connections. And the other side of the coin matters too: who do you want in your network? There's likely to be different layers to this, but it's important to take the time to understand who you're hoping to add to your network at any given time. Potential co-founders? Mentors or advisors? Investors? Peers? People with specific skills? By understanding both who they are and what you can offer, you can get a handle on how you approach conversations.

A very simple way to do this is to literally write down, on a piece of paper or in a document, what you can offer. Next, in a list alongside it, write down with whom you want to strengthen your connection. Then, think of ways to make the first list appealing to the second, both as a whole and individually. This gives you an 'in' and a practical way to start building your tribe. To return to the key point of this question – maintenance – it also gives you a simple starting point for maintaining the network over time. If you repeat this exercise over the months and years (in lieu of any other natural connections that keep your network connections fresh – we call this 'engineering serendipity', and you can read more about it later in this chapter), you'll always have a simple strategy for contacting the people you want to keep close.

Of course, there are also people who will come into your life that you aren't targeting. This is great! But in these cases, it's even more important to have a clear strategy for maintaining their presence in your network. It can be very similar to the strategy outlined above, but with the simple addition of determining whether it is someone you want to keep in your network or just someone you had a nice chat with. There are, after all, only so many hours in the day. But we would counsel that if you can see a connection having value at any time in the future, then it's worth putting the effort in. It may just be a gut feeling rather than something calculated, but that's okay too. We're humans, not robots. But be sure that, if you're embarking on this journey, you understand the importance of building and maintaining what you've got.

It's about mindset

If you're in the mindset of maintaining a network, then you're 90% of the way there. Maintenance is something that happens because of effort put in over the years, and, like compound interest, it really starts to bite as time goes on. Having a long-term view allows you to harness the power of this compounding so you can take control of your time and energy and feel confident that your networking activities will deliver results over time. It also, by extension, means that others have a long-term relationship with you. This means they know you better, you know them better and you can both be better at supporting each other.

Another useful mindset to have when maintaining a network is vulnerability. It's okay to ask for help. It's okay to show where you're weaker. It's okay to be brutally honest about what you're doing, how it's going and what's not going so well. In fact, these things are not only okay, they're important. Not just for our own mental health but because, deep down, most people are driven to help others. It's part of the trade-off of also being able to seek help when you need it. If you genuinely need help, then ask. If you are in a position to offer help, then do. This is really the engine that's powering the whole business world.[23]

With 9others, we've always been clear that people can come to dinners as often as they like. It's not a case of coming along, getting some ideas and then disappearing. This is, in part, because we want to strengthen our connections with people in

23 Good people want to help you; it's that simple. By being vulnerable, you will find out very quickly who you can rely on and who isn't going to be there for you. It's an easy filter that moves you forward more quickly and with more accuracy.

that network, but it's also because we genuinely want to help them – if that's what they need.

Sometimes, people come to a few in a row (such as Chris Sheldrick, founder of what3words, who came to several dinners as they were launching back in 2013), while some come back years later. Patrick Walsh came to a dinner when we started writing this book but hadn't been to one since 2015! Another person at that same dinner was Mike Bandar, who had never been to a 9others dinner before but had been on the mailing list since Matthew had (unsuccessfully!) tried to sell him a desk in his King's Cross co-working space in 2013.

Maintenance of your network will pay off, but it's hard work.

Here are some practical tips to help:

- Have a regular check-in point to meet with key people. Agree on a time/date/location that works and stick to it. It could be weekly, monthly or less often if that suits, too, and it could change over time/with needs.
- Set regular days to go through older contacts and decide which need reigniting. Be curious about what people you met a while back are doing now. Dig out old emails and ask them!
- Respond quickly to people you care about. The aim should be immediately, the default within 24 hours.
- Be open and acknowledge if you don't know the answer to something or can't help. People may come to you for answers, but it's okay not to know. Even if you do have a pretty clear idea, you should certainly not tell people exactly what to do. It's about each of us finding our own way.

- Learn how people want to engage. Sadly, there's not one universal messaging system, so some people prefer WhatsApp over email, DM on Twitter/Instagram/ LinkedIn/Slack, and even use phone calls. They can seem the same, but for whatever reason different people respond to different messages. It feels like a secret superpower to know that you can DM someone on Twitter and get a response when the rest of the world is emailing them and getting nowhere.
- Remembering the odd thing about someone can make a huge difference. When so many people are transactional, remembering that someone likes a particular hobby or remembering something about their family, home town or sports team (good or bad!) can create a much more solid connection that they will remember long after you forget it.
- Always be respectful of everyone and treat everyone the same. You'll come across some people you might think are more successful, richer, more renowned, but they're just people too. At 9others there's no hierarchy – students just starting out have sat next to millionaires. People like it because there's no bravado and no nonsense: everyone is there to contribute, and everyone is there to learn.

The maintenance manifesto

Maintaining your connections is important to build real momentum in your network. Keep in mind the following whenever this feels tough:

- It's okay to do short check-ins (just keep them interesting and authentic).

- It's okay to disappear for a bit (everyone's busy and life has a habit of getting in the way).
- It's okay to get back in touch with someone after several months or even years (people like it!).

The point here is to deal with the anxiety that can be caused by thinking you need to keep in touch with everyone, all the time. This isn't possible and, most importantly, it isn't necessary.

One way to better square your energy with maintaining connections is to think about how 'deep rooted' your relationship goes. People whom we've known for years and built great trust with can go much longer between conversations without any real dip in the connection. On the other hand, you would most likely find it a bit odd if somebody you met ten years ago got in touch to say hello out of the blue, although if they had something very valuable and targeted to say and you remembered that meeting fondly (even with a bit of a reminder), then would it be so odd? As ever, it goes back to being clear about what value you're giving, as well as what you hope to receive.

Serendipity

A final word on the role of serendipity in maintaining a network. It's important to engineer serendipity, by which we mean 'make sure that random things happen'. What you don't want is some artificial intelligence to take away that serendipity and push you into echo chambers or deep furrows of all-too-similar connections. This is where your human spirit comes in and where you can break all the rules we've just outlined to see what happens.

Great stories always have some serendipity in them. Your favourite book or film almost certainly relies on it. If you want to write your own great story as you build your business, then you need to have some too. Good ways to do this are to go to new/strange/different places or events; try new routes home or to work; sit somewhere different; ask different questions; say hello to people in strange situations; strike up conversations (in a respectful way, of course) on transport, while walking the dog or while out for a run; change plans at the last minute; get on the wrong bus; contact a random number or email address; respond to every opportunity no matter how odd and much more. You'll have your own limits, of course, but embrace the serendipity, and trust that a leap of faith often leads to good things.

From the dinner table

When building Qatalog I was able to draw on connections from previous roles I'd held at Wise and Amazon and relationships with people from other established companies. This has made for a team of experienced individuals and a great source of talent. I didn't think about this exact scenario while I was working in these companies and didn't note colleagues as potential future employees. I really enjoy working with driven and motivated people and seek them out as much as possible. This has been of substantial help in the process of building an ambitious startup.

– Tariq Rauf, Qatalog

Generating social currency through generosity makes asking for help graciously possible and, as an introvert, I know I have to take good care of my network to do this. Most of us introverts would rather shove hot needles into our eyeballs than go to a 'networking event', but I have found attending 9others and hosting smaller dinners different, and safer, for the 'socially quieter'.

– Alex Knapp, founder and CEO of AKC Global

Maintaining a network is something that I've always seen as of paramount importance to my life and career, but probably not for the reasons you'd expect. Network for me is all about being able to give back, provide opportunities and build the 'network effect'. Whilst I have, of course, benefitted from having an extensive network, the joy I get from connecting people together or providing opportunities via my network is huge. Often the benefit to you only comes from years of giving first into communities without any expectation in return. So if you only view your network as of value to yourself, then you miss out on the opportunity to see the value and opportunity you yourself can have to the broader community. I've been able to support people's career changes, provide advice on starting businesses, connect female founders together and more, which in turn has allowed those people to pay it forward and provide value through their network.

Building and maintaining a great network for me requires three key things: authenticity, engagement and a genuine interest in the other person. Starting with authenticity, this requires me bringing my whole self to conversations, moving away from transactional relationships and really connecting with people. It also means having the courage to face difficult conversations when needed to ensure you maintain good relationships. When I had the unenviable task of closing down my own startup, I had to inform our investors of the investment position (spoiler: it wasn't positive news!). I had heard people manage these situations in a few ways, from emails to phone calls to sitting on a beach taking a Zoom call (the last one is not advised). However, I had been so grateful and had the utmost respect for what our investors had done for us and the connections they had made and help they had given. As such, to me it was absolutely critical I took each meeting face to face. They were some of the most difficult conversations I've ever had, but it allowed me to continue a truly authentic connection and show that I didn't run away from such difficult conversations. In the end, maintaining the authenticity of those relationships led one of my investors to connect me with my next career opportunity. Whilst that is one example, I often hear the great networkers I know talk about how similar difficult situations have ensured they stay true to their values and maintain authenticity with connections, allowing them to build more trusted and impactful relationships beyond the initially difficult part.

Second, it's important to maintain engagement with your network but, as above, keep it authentic and relevant. Engagement isn't about reaching out for the sake of reaching out because you feel you have to; it is all about why you are connecting. It's about sitting in conversations and thinking how you can be helpful to that person for no other reason than you could be a little piece of that person's next adventure. When I worked at Techstars our mantra was 'give first', which we all truly lived and breathed. That focus on giving without the expectation of anything in return allowed us to build and maintain a powerful global network. I had the privilege of meeting fantastic community leaders through Techstars, one of which I was able to stay in touch with to provide mentoring support at events. Eventually that individual went on to start their own business where I was able to join as an advisor. After several years, my journey took me to launch an office in the US. I reached out to connect and ended up meeting several senior leadership connections via that person. Good engagement doesn't have a set cadence; it is much more about supporting your network in the best way you can.

Finally, to maintain a good network you need to have genuine interest in the other person. This ties together both authenticity and engagement. To build a well-connected network you have to believe in the other person's journey and want to know more about them. To be a great connector you have to really know the people in your network. Not only does this allow you to see the connection opportunities you can provide, but it gives you the opportunity to trade ideas and collaboration opportunities and understand each person's skills. Over time this brings exponential impact to what your network can be and allows you to connect in a meaningful way. I've had the opportunity to work globally through opportunities provided to me within my network. Through that work I've connected with individuals from all walks of life. I have been so fascinated by those individuals' journeys that I have genuinely wanted to support and learn from them as much as I can. These connections have profoundly impacted the diversity of my thinking and therefore how I've built my network. My network has been built through my career but also by connecting through shared experiences, from global hackathons to attending 9others with a huge range of individuals.

When I was asked to answer this question by Matthew, it made me smile. Matthew, Katie and 9others exemplify the key tenets of building a great network and have been a key part of my journey. As the 9others mission goes, 'Your success requires the aid of others.' My success has been defined by the network I've had around me, but more than that it has made me grateful to be someone who can 'aid' others' adventures. There is so much joy in building a great network, and you never know where it may take you; for me right now the next stop is a wedding in Panama!

– Lauren Hine, chief of hub operations at AND Digital

Conclusion

Maintaining your network is a skill in itself. While it can feel as if the core skill in 'networking' is meeting new people and upping the numbers, those in the know understand that it's really about the nurturing.

There's no getting away from the fact that it's hard work maintaining a network, but fortunately you can approach it in a structured way. Use the practical tips in this chapter to do a little maintenance work every single day and you'll see the value of your network grow in ways you never imagined.

Your network is a living, breathing thing. Treat it as such, and don't let it die.

Questions to ask of yourself and others

Which of the practical tips from this chapter am I going to commit to? Networking is a very personal activity, and you need to find the ways it works for you. We've outlined a lot of practical advice in this chapter, so go back over it and pick out the things that really resonate (and start doing them!).

Which of the practical tips from this chapter did I ignore because they scare me? Yeah, you're probably going to need to do those too. But it'll be worth it.

Question 10
Can I do it all on my own?

To innovate is to play, to take an idea and bounce it around the court, throw it to different people and ask, 'What if…?' And I love that – especially when it's not our own challenge to solve.
– Sarah Ticho, founder of Hatsumi

Your success requires the aid of others.

As much as some people believe that if a job's worth doing, it's worth doing themselves, we very much disagree. As we proudly proclaim to all who attend 9others dinners, your success requires the aid of others. For us, that means several things. It means you need people to help you, buy from you, fund you, work with you, counsel you, mentor you, coach you and no doubt more. It means you need others. It means you cannot succeed alone.

Aligned with this we have another strong belief: the best way to get help is to give it.

If you're helpful, generous, kind and available – all without the expectation of something in exchange – then others will be drawn to help you too. Not all of them, of course. Some will take advantage or have nothing of use to offer in return. But that's a fine price to pay for all the good that authentic, meaningful help provides. One, it feels good. Two, you learn things and develop your own skills doing stuff. Three, you identify those who are worth getting to know better and those worth avoiding.

As we touched on in the previous chapters, giving reveals what other people are like and uncovers if they're the people you want to start and build a relationship with. It also shows whether you can trust them. One thing that's true of life is that, eventually, everyone will show you who they are – you just have to wait. If you give regularly, then you'll realize quicker and won't have to wait for someone you've invested time and energy in to reveal themselves. Specifically, you can learn if people think, 'What else can I get from this person?' or 'What can I do in return?' This also highlights the good people earlier, of course, and from there you can choose where to focus your time and energy.

Banking it

When you do a good deed, we think it's useful to consider it as part of the 'bank balance' we first outlined in Question 8, another bottom line you want to keep an eye on as you go about growing your business. When you need something, you're at liberty to take a withdrawal from that 'bank'. But, as with any account, you don't want it to run to zero. You want a healthy bank balance in case you ever need to make any emergency withdrawals, and you really don't want to go into the red. It's a helpful metaphor, we find, as most people are familiar with the issues that would come from not having enough cash in the bank.

Something you may note here is that needing others in this kind of ecosystem goes against the dog-eat-dog narrative of business as a competitive, unreasonable or even horrible place to operate. Truth is, while that may make for some juicy headlines and complex fictional characters, the most successful businesspeople get on because they know how to be part of a healthy ecosystem built on exchange and respect. Indeed, if you look at the world's most successful founders and businesspeople, then you'll notice something they all have in common – they bring people with them. They lift people up, and people follow them. They provide for others, and others provide for them. There are, of course, myriad variables that determine who ends up 'on top', or richest or most revered, but none of that comes without a healthy network of helpers.

Give to get

You probably use Google. The funny thing about Google is that, when you go to ask it for help, it sends you away somewhere even more useful. That's kind of odd, isn't it? A business that is built to send you away to other places. But it works. It's one of the most dominant brands in the world because it works. When you want to find something again, you go back to Google. And the more it works, the more you embed it in your life.

With 9others, when we thought about this, something clicked. At one point we were wondering if there was a way to generate value from connections we make. What if we connect people who go off to make $100 million and we get no direct benefit from it? Thing is, we're not in that business; we're not a broker always looking for a cut. If we were, then 9others wouldn't have lasted five minutes. Or at least it would be an ongoing struggle. But by connecting people together, we've built something different and interesting, and people keep coming back. They keep coming to help others (and help us out too).

For Google, its core business is search, not content, and that's why it works. Of course, it has gone far beyond that now, but its foundation of trust helped the company do that.

You see, the only thing that differentiates your business is you and the way you work. Others will offer solutions to the same problems and be on a similar mission or have look-a-like products, but your ethos, your desire for a certain reputation and your effort to be known for something specific mark you out. In a world where skills are common and increasingly commoditized, it's attitude that really sets you apart.

In the context of aiding others, that attitude is one of giving back – to customers, to partners, to investors, to staff and to society. If you're focused on doing that, then you will be seen in a good light. Sure, we can't all give the millions that Bezos, Gates or Buffett do, but why do you think they do it?[24] If we want things to happen, whatever the level and whatever the context, then the best way to get them is to give more. More of our money, maybe, if that's what we're overflowing with, but

[24] We'll let you decide how cynical you want to be on this one.

also more of ourselves, more of our ideas, more of our insights, more of our connections.

If you're sitting there, after all this, thinking, 'What if karma doesn't play its role for me and things *don't* come back?' Well, at least others have benefitted. Isn't that better than nobody benefitting and no chance of support coming your way?

From the dinner table

Let me tell you about the Old Man of Shanidar. Rewind, if you don't mind, through just your last 24 hours. There'll be an instance, however big or small, where you needed help but didn't ask for it. Cooperation is baked into our DNA. Our shared human story, now lasting hundreds of thousands of years, is the longest of anthologies that has shown time and time again that we're at our beautiful best when greater than the sum of our individual parts. No baby, no technical innovation, no newly discovered shore or avoided war has ever happened without this crazy-magical-sparkling-collaborative something that results from one person combining minds and hearts with another or, with exponential truth, multiple and diverse others. Isn't it a paradox, then, that, despite our obvious, daily reliance on those around us (and our very existence to prove this is a good thing), we rarely turn to the person closest to us in a moment of need and say four simple words, 'Can you help me?' Here's the thing: it's not (only) about you.

When it comes to underestimating those around us, we've got a bit of form, us Homo sapiens. Until recently, we've projected a very particular view onto our closest relatives, the Neanderthals. Brutish, stupid, lesser versions of ourselves, what could we possibly learn from them bar the odd interesting anthropological tooling discovery? In hobbles the Old Man of Shanidar…

Discovered in the late 1950s within a cave amidst a mountainous area of modern-day Iraq, 'Nandy', as he became known to his excavators, displayed clear signs of deformity most likely caused by trauma well before his death date. Skull and ear canal injuries show his later years were likely lived mostly blind and deaf, and a withered, fractured arm led at least to a total loss of arm and hand mobility but may have also impacted, presumably through nerve damage, the physical abnormalities found in his lower legs and feet. Clearly, Nandy's survival was dependent on the support and compassion of those who cared for and supported him. Why? Well, here's where my job as an internet blogger ends and the job of our world-leading anthropologists begins. But at the very least, the Old Man of Shanidar tells me that, when it comes to needing help, there's something in it for both sides. In 2013 I started my blog with a simple offer of help to anyone who needed it; if I could help, I said, I would help for free and do so anonymously. I received thousands of responses, and by far the most common was 'Can I help you help others?' So the next time you're in need of help, please consider this an opportunity for someone to fulfil their need to do what they can for you. But be warned, it starts with that simple question you rarely ask: 'Can you help me?'

– Tom Cledwyn, The Free Help Guy

'If you want to go fast, go alone. If you want to go far, go together.' What a lonely existence it would be to create and build alone. My work has always been about interdisciplinary thinking, inviting in new approaches, new ways of being and innovating. As an anthropologist by training, I think much of my early career was about exploring the different ways that people exist within and experience the world, and having a diversity of opinion and perspective always strengthens the products we're building. To innovate is to play, to take an idea and bounce it around the court, throw it to different people and ask, 'What if…?' And I love that – especially when it's not our own challenge to solve. This is Solomon's Paradox: it is always easier

to solve each other's problems than our own. No matter how big or small the problem, just being heard and talking it out always helps. I have learned so much about myself and reframed my challenges by listening to others, and I equally believe that others helping me has also benefitted them in seeing their own challenges in a new light.

– Sarah Ticho, founder of Hatsumi

I just got back from a five-day workshop on improvisational drama. In its purest form, you walk on to an empty stage with no plan or script and try to make an audience really feel something.

This would be fucking terrifying and basically impossible to do on your own. When you first start improvising, you imagine that it requires acts of herculean imagination and cerulean-sky creativity. But the audience can feel that immediately as a desperate grasping at empty air. Instead, any performance that works comes from outside our head. You need to be ever-so-aware of and curious about your fellow performers, to treat their every word and movement as clues and seeds. In responding as truthfully as you can to them, building incrementally on what they offer by yes-anding their reality, you find yourself somewhere none of you could have imagined, and yet collectively you did. It is so very joyful to surprise oneself, but, paradoxically, you need other people to do it.

– Greg Detre, Filtered

Conclusion

You can have everything in life you want, if you will just help other people get what they want.[25]

– Zig Ziglar

---

[25] K. Kruse, 'Zig Ziglar: 10 quotes that can change your life', *Forbes* (28 November 2012). Available from: www.forbes.com/ sites/ kevinkruse/2012/11/28/zig-ziglar-10-quotes-that-can-change-your-life/?sh=3d4c1dfb26a0

We live in a world of algorithms, robots and artificial intelligence. They're examining emails and other messages, tracking open rates and times, and scanning cursors and eyeballs to better understand how to get the perfect broadcast message to us so we'll take some particular action. While there may be some argument to be made for the benefits of this at scale in certain situations, we wouldn't want you to forget about unpredictable, quirky, eccentric human aspects as a way to help you grow your business and drive towards your mission.

A key part of this is the reality that you simply can't second guess what will be of value or interest to people. All you can do is put things in front of them and see if they lead anywhere, which you'll never truly know because, as we've discussed already, things can take time; they can be part of a relationship that blossoms many years later. This is what keeps the energy and creates the buzz when you just help people because it's what you do.

So this is where this book has been leading. Know who you are, know what you're trying to do and go out there and start talking to people. It will make you tougher, it will make you more determined and it will help you, and your business, improve and grow.

A strong network, well maintained and fuelled by your own desire to help make a difference to the fortune of others, is something special. But only because it's hard and requires focus and dedication. Not everyone has a great network, but you can.

After all, your success requires the aid of others, ***your*** *others.*

Questions to ask of yourself and others

Who am I going to help today? It's that simple. Pick someone and offer your help. It might be the start of something beautiful or it might not, but you won't know unless you try.

How am I going to help them? It could be an act of kindness, sharing some useful information in an email or just something they'd enjoy. It might be big; it might be small. It just needs to happen.

How can I make helping people a habit? Do you need a timetable or checklist to help you? Are there certain groups that you know you can regularly support? Is there something specific – finding customers for others or introducing new hires, for example – that you can do over and over?

Thank you

Thank you for reading our book.

We hope you've found lots of inspiration in these pages, but most of all we hope you know exactly what you're going to do next. Because that's really the point. It's up to you now to take these lessons from the extended 9others network and put them into practice.

On the next page you'll find the chapter titles in one simple list. Think of it as a manifesto; a simple guide to the lessons we've shared. Rip it out, pin it up somewhere, annotate it as you go. Don't be precious – we're not.

If you liked this book, please tell people about it. Word of mouth is the most potent marketing. And if you really liked it, you can visit our website at 9others.com to buy another copy for someone who wouldn't otherwise be able to afford it.

The trick to being a successful founder (and 9others)

Question 1: Why am I doing this, anyway?

Question 2: How do I get more visible?

Question 3: What do I do with my gut reactions?

Question 4: How do I keep getting up again?

Question 5: What does it take to succeed?

Question 6: How do I get comfortable being uncomfortable?

Question 7: What does success look like?

Question 8: Who can help?

Question 9: How do I keep the right people around me?

Question 10: Can I do it all on my own?

Thanks to everyone who has been to a meal with 9others in the first ten years*:

Taru Aalto
Ben Abbott
Tristan Abbott
Larissa Abbud
Ed Abis
Abotalb
Rob Abrahams
Adil Abrar
Abrika
Chris Acheson
Benn Achilleas
Jeremy Acklam
Andreas Adamides
Barry Adams
Joy Adams
Luke Adams
Matt Adams
Darryl Addie
Sophie Adelman
Oooota Adepo
David Adesanya
Martin Ahe
Christian Ahlert
Waqar Ahmed
Peter Aitsi
Richard Aked
William Akerman
Askin Akhan
Dele Akinyemi
Oleksandr Akymenko
Naz Alatli
Adrian Alcantara Martinez
Kat Alder
Hector Alexander
Victor Alexiev
Christian Alhert
Aysha Ali
Aman Allawala
Catherine Allen
David Allen
Karl Allen
James Allsopp
Fabrizia Alonzo
Yusra Alshahari
Luca Amaduzzi
Sade Amale
Ashok Amaran
Mithra Amaran
Jonny Ambrose
Alissa Ananieva
Arman Anaturk
Michaela Anchan
Anna Anderson
Geoff Anderson
Nathan Anderson
Trace Anderson
Emanuel Andjelic
Sara Anjargolian
Tom Ansell
Ksenija Apena
Jehan Ara Ali
Nadia Arain
Narek Aramjan
Kosta Ard Sam
Andrew Arias
Oleksiy Aristov
Wicastr Llc
Armine Saidi
Guy Armitage
Tim Armoo
Becks Armstrong
Meelimari Arro
Steven Arthur
Pru Ashby
Oliver Ashness
Jonathan Ashong-Lamptey
Bassil Aslam
Kashif Aslam
Souad-Marie Assaad
Kophong Assawachaiwasin
Sandra Astrom
Dele Atanda

Jon Atkinson
Sarah Atkinson
Arman Atoyan
Paul Attard
Gordon Au
Enbar Averbukh
Leon Averbukh
Joe Averill
Sally Averill
Janet Awe
Muz Azar
Maeen Aziz
Cenk Baban
Alyce Babauskis
Carrie Babcock
David Back
Vittorio Badalassi
River Baig
Daniel Bailey
David Bailey
Dawn Baird
Piotr Bajtała
Brad Baker
Arka Bala
James Banc
Zenona
Bańkowska
John Banks
Filippo Barberis
Ricardo Barcellos
Manuhuia
Barcham
Dave Barcos
Stephen Bardle
Ben Barker
Daisy Barnes
Paul Barnes
Claudia
Barriga-Larriviere
Jonathan
Barrowman
Piotr Barszczewski
Joe Bartleet
Amy Basil
Bernard Baskin
Tom Bass
Daniel Batchelor
Michael Bateman
Stuart Bates
Paul Batterham
Stuart Battersby
David Battey
Dan Bauer
Chris Baxter
Aurelien Bayer
Antonia Bayly
Samir Bayraktar
Charlotte Bearn
John Beckett
Seonaid Beckwith
Shona Beckwith
Dan Bedi
Chris Beech
Nicholas Begley
Kevin Beimers
Andy Bell
Douglas Bell
Rachel Bell
Elodie Bellegarde
Melissa Belongea
Arielle Benadi
Amir Bendjazia
Harry Bennett
Mia Bennett
Adrien Bennings
Peter Benson
Ryan Benson
Will Bentinck
Natalia
Berezovska
Alex Berezovskiy
Nel Berezowska-
Lewicka
Imogen Berman
Romans Bermans
Vincent Berndsen
Frank Bertele
Julien Berthomier
Victoria Betton
Mike Betts
Colin Beveridge
Sanjay Bhiraju
Swetha Bhupathi
Philipp Bieberstein
Tom Bielecki
Damian Bieniek
David Biggs
Alexis Biller
Paul Billington

Freddy Billowes
Emma Bindbeutel
Andrew Binnendijk
Yael Biran
Greg Birmingham
Maximilian Birner
James Bishop
Joel Biswas
Samit Biswas
Jonathan Blackwell
Matthew Blakemore
Francois Blanc
Paul Blanchard
Magnus Blikeng
Adam Bloodworth
Charley Bloodworth
Martin Bloom
Wayne Bloore
Charlie Bloxham
Hamish Blythe
Amelia Boadle
Francesca Boccolini
Nick Boddington
Kate Boeckman
Tim Boeckmann
Matt Boffey
Josh Bolland
Phil Bolton
Chris Bond
Dmytro Bondar
Tatyana Bondarchuk
Petro Bondarevskyi
Arnaud Bonzom
David Boon
David Booth
Gergely Borgulya
Dustin Botha
Henriette Botha
Francois Bouet
Bianca Bovell
Andrew Bowd
David Bowker
David Bowler
Danielle Bowman
Stuart Bowness
Dan Bowyer
Jamie Boyle
David Boyo
Andrew Brackin
Jessica Bradley
Joel Bramwell
Heike Brandt
Isabelle Brennan
Richard Brett
Matthew Briars
James Bridgman
David Briggs
Luke Briner
Gerard Briscoe
Adam Britton
Alexandra Brodie
Ian Broom
Sally Broom
Lauren Broomhall
Eric Brotto
Ben Brown
Christopher Brown
David Brown
Francis Brown
Jim Brown
Karina Brown
Richard Brown
George Brownlee
Mark Bruce
Lukas Bruell
Anne Bruinvels
Daniele Bruttini
Michael Bruvel
Tom Bryan
Adam Buchan
Nick Buckley
Hawaa Budraa
Dillon Buirski
Jacques Bulchand
Christopher Bull
Antony Bullivant
Andriy Burenok
Richard Burge
David Burgess
George Burgess
Mirek Burkon
Jess Butcher

Luke Byrne
Fred Caballero
Gabbi Cahane
Don Cai
Lucia Caistor
David Calap
Danny Callan
Richard Cambridge
Neil Cameron
Marco Camisanicalzolari
Cristiana Camisotti
David Campbell
Mark Cann
Stephen Canning
Ashley Cao
Ben Carey
Grace Carey
Mark Carnighan
Andrew Carr
Richard Carrick
Leigh Carrick-Moore
James Carroll
Dominic Carter
Josh Carter
Luciana Carvalho Se
Emily Casey
Nikola Cavic
Laima Cekule
Chloe Celand
Tristan Celder
Alessandro Cerrone
Karan Chadda
Jean-Michel Chalayer
Tani Chambers
Barak Chamo
Bernard Chan
Trae Chancellor
Gerard Chandrahasen
Jeffrey Chang
Paul Chapman
Duncan Chapple
Anastasia Charalabidou
Leesa Charlotte
Andy Charlton
Christopher Chave-Cox
Ishete Chellaiah
Kevin Chen
Renee Chen
Limiao Cheng
Evgeny Chernikov
Darius Cheung
Maxim Chevalier
Silaporn Chiawwicha
Julian Childs
Aravindan Chinnaraja
Vin Chinnaraja
Krista Chism
Paulina Chodnicka
Tasha Choi
Vincent Choi
Ewa Chojecka
Shaf Choudry
Louise Chow
Raees Chowdhury
Yingqun Christina Cao
Jake Christoforou
Conno Christou
Vincent Chu
Nipatpong Chuanchuen
Edwin Chung
Grace Clapham
Adrian Clark
Barnaby Clark
Lewis Clark
Sam Clark
Tina Clark
Tom Cledwyn
Elen Clement
Rachel Clemo
Claire Clerkin
Randal Cliff
Dee Coakley
David Cobb
Oliver Codrington
Bill Cogan
Alistair Cohen

Elad Cohen
Jodie Cole
Scott Coleman
Andrew Collinson
Marco Colombo
Alex Colonna
Thubten Comerford
Chris Connell
Peter Connolly
Chip Conrad
Andrew Conru
Andrea Consonni
Ruskin Constant
Shifra Cook
Stuart Cook
Chelsea Cooper
Jenny Cooper
Scott Cooper
Rachel Cope
Daniel Copeland
Marc Corbalan
Simon Corbett
Heather Corcoran
Florian Cornu
Jon Cornwell
James Corpe
Michael Correa
Marc Costafreda
Matthew Cottingham
Sean Cottrell
Elliot Cowan
Toni Cowan-Brown
William Cowell De Gruchy
Tina Cowen
David Cox
Ellenor Cox
Linda Coyle
Daniel Crawford
Paul Crayston
Timothy Creswick
Ian Crocombe
Justin Cross
Olga Crosse
Allistair Crossley
Cristina Crucianu
Andrew Crump
Andreas Cser
Michele Cuccovillo
Dominic Cudmore
Victoria Cullen
Oliver Cummings
Ian Cunningham
Zoe Cunningham
Patrick Curtis
Dominik Cymer
Gaurav Dudhoria
Chris D'Aloisio
Adam D'Souza
Małgorzata Dąbkowska
Debbie Dahan
Anna Dahlstrom
Alex Daish
Clelia Dal Col
Robbie Dale
Jeremy Dalton
Ken Damien
Taha Dar
Tim Davey
Schehrezade Davidson
Ben Davies
Jon Davies
Laura Davies
Maxie Davies
Tom Davis
Kevin De Baere
Xavier De Lecaros-Aquise
Marco De Nichilo
Bart De Smet
Christian De Stefani
Tielman De Villiers
Phillippa De'Ath
James Deakin
Caroline Dean
Patrick Deba
Eleanor Deeley
Kateryna Dehtyar
Volodymyr Dehtyarov
Itxaso Del Palacio

Charlie Delingpole
Deval Delivala
Sarah Dembitz
Dermot Dennehy
Marley Dennis
Greg Detre
Grant Dewar
Rajeeb Dey
Federico Diato
Ricardo Diaz Lombardo
Bronie Dickson
Casey Dilloway
Leigh Dixon
Kimberley Dobney
Maciek Dobrowolski
Graham Dockrill
Amy Doherty
Richard Doherty
Camilla Dolan
James Donaghy
Matt Donazzan
Veronique Dong
Andrea Donoso
Karl Doran
Matthew Doran
Mitchell Dorman
Rafael Dos Santos
Sarthak Doshi
Andrew Douglas
Ross Douglas
Jane Dowling
Charlotte Downs
Toby Downton
Ian Dowson
Sinead Doyle
Maren Goerdel
Pred Dragila
Adam Dreiblatt
Monika Drozdzikowska
Paul Drury
Johann Du Bruyn
Arnold Du Toit
Alex Dubsdon
Yuriy Dubyk
Alain Duchesne
Gaurav Dudhoria
Peter Duffy
Sean Dukes
Michael Dulchin
Brett Duncan
Alex Dunsdon
Elena Duran
Michał Durski
Isaiah Duty
Oleksandr Dzyuba
Christopher Easton
Mike Ebinum
Dean Economou
James Eder
Ben Edge
Craig Edmunds
Adam Edwards
Sam Edwards
Stuart Eggleton
Ekow Eghan
Louise Eldridge
Bianca Elgar
Tas Elias
Jonny Elliott
Andrew Ellis
Guy Ellis
Andrey Emelyanenko
Will Emmett
Annika Erikson
Safak Erkol
Jeroen Erne
Jeremy Ervine
Alejandro Escoda
Pepe Escuredo
Bec Evans
Cerith Evans
Debbi Evans
Joshua Evans
Craig Everett
Adam Ewart
Paul Excell
Robyn Exton
Harry Fairhead
Djoann Fal
Michael Fangman
Paolo Farinella
Dustin Farivar
Elijah Farley

Alexandra Farmer
James Farmer
Hadi Farnoud
Neil Farnworth
George Farquhar
David Farquharson
Alexander Farrell
David Fauchier
Anwar Fazla
Roland Felber
Jade Feng
Jordi Fernandez
Maria Fernandez
Ruark Ferreira
Paul Field
Magdalena Filcek
Penny Fillhouer
Michael Fillié
Heloise Finch-Boyer
Elaine Finn
Alex Finnemore
Nikki Finnemore
Alfonso Fiore
Mo Firouzabadian
Ben Fisher
Hercules Fisherman
Zane Fitch
Sheri Fitts
Nikki Fiveash
Kevin Flanagan
Sophie Fleming
Ben Fletcher
Mark Fletcher
Emma Forster
Faith Forster
Drew Forsyth
Rosemary Forsyth
Lisa Fox
Anthony Fox-Davies
Marty Foy
Tiago Franco
Zebedee Franklin
Kenny Fraser
Nick Freer
Isabelle Freidheim
Geir Freysson
Iliya Fridman
Vivi Friedgut
Vladimir Frolov
Nina Froriep
Daren Fuchs
Alexander Furey
Kirsty Ilona Furniss
Richard Gahagan
Rajdeep Gahir
David Galbraith
Brian Gale
Matthew Gale
Marta Galewska
Bob Gallagher
Michelle Gallen
Marion Gamel
Galit Gan
Iqbal Gandham
Virginia Gardiner
Alex Gardner
Stuart Gardner
George Garnham
Chris Garrett
Kathleen Garrett
Tomer Garzberg
Matthew Gass
Ben Gateley
Saranta Gattie
Leon Gauhman
Yiannis Gavrielides
Rachel Gawley
Mark Gazki
Christian Geissendoerfer
Anthony Gell
Sam Gellman
Andy Gent
Hristo Georgiev
Oleg Gerasimenko
Mike Gibbs
David Gielty
Adam Gieniusz
Shai Gilat
David Gilbeh
Liam Gilchrist
Patrick Gilday
David Gildeh

Daniel Gill
Doireann Gillan
J R Gillespie
Sean Gilmour
Kelly Gilmour-Grassam
Grace Gimson
Eni Gjondedaj
Dan Glazer
Lucie Glenday
Meli Glenn
Regina Glenn
Rosa Glover
Katherine Goddard
Richard Gold
Judy Goldberg
Seth Goldstein
Jonny Goldstone
Alexey Golev
Kateryna Golianych
Krzysztof Goliński
Roman Gonitel
Adam Goodall
Marc Goodchild
Richard Goold
Rachel Goor
Elle Gormley
Konrad Gotlib
Antonio Gould
Meeta Gournay
Alex Gowar
Samridh Goyal
Dmitri Grabov
Magda Grabowska
John Graham
Joshua Graham
Louise Graham
Richard Graham
Kyle Grant
Alex Gray
Andrew Gray
Heather Gray
Gerard Grech
Jason Greenberg
Adam Greene
Brett Greene
Richard Gregory
Ugne Greivyte
Jules Griffi th
Cordelia Griffi ths
Gemma Griffi ths
Nicholas Grime
Mark Grimes
Allen Grimm
Tatiana Grinuova
Valentin Gritsenko
Sally Guelfi
Juan Guerra
David Guerra
Terol
Alex Guest
Kim Guest
Phil Guest
Kimberly Guiry
Rico Gujjula
Joanne Gunn
Matthew Gunn
Dmitry Gyk
Janne Gylling
Sylvia Ha
John Haggis
Andrew Haigh
Simon Halberstam
Suzie Halewood
Dan Hall
Daniel Hall
Peter Hames
Matthew Hammett
Ian Hammond
John Hampson
Tiffany Handley
Jazz Hanley
Anthony Hanna
Damian Hanson
Hans Hanspal
Farid Haque
Elly Hardwick
James Harford-Tyrer
Kit Hargreaves
Christine Harmel
Laura Harnett
Sadia Haroon
Dave Harper
Craig Harries
Julie Harris

Keith Harris
Will Harris
Andrew Hart
Colleen Harte
Sally Hartfi eld
Alexander Harutunian
Roland Harwood
Seasan Hashmi
Rosie Haslem
Basil Hassan
Syed Hassan
Tatu Hautala
Lee Hawkins
James Haycock
Raj Hayer
Caroline Hayward
Ian Hayward
Vincent Haywood
Tsepo Headbush
Michael Healy
Richard Heap
Alex Heaton
Johan Hedin
Sebastian Heinz
Nigel Helen
Nigel Hembrow
Michael Henderson
Alan Heppenstall
Nicky Herbert
Paul Herdemian
Shane Herft
Lennart Hergel
Nitzan Hermon
Iker Hernandez
Juan Herrada
Tom Hickman
Valerie Higgins
Catherine Highet
Alexandra Hilker
Christian Hill
Gilbert Hill
Serenity Hill
Emily Hilton
Jonathan Himoff
Lauren Hine
Will Hines
Volker Hirsch
Jana Hlistova
Angel Ho
Nick Hoang
Ben Hoban
Stephen Hobson
Clement Hochart
Andy Hodgetts
Tim Hodgkinson
Will Hodson
Kris Hofmann
Chris Hogg
Domini Hogg
Lee Holdsworth
Sam Holguin
Archie Hollingsworth
Lisa Hollinshead
Dan Holloway
Mathew Holloway
Robert Holmkvist
Garth Holsinger
Braden Holt
Jonathan Holtby
Richard Homer
Andrew Honneysett
Juan Hontanilla
Heloise Hooton
Asa Hope
Tom Hopkins
Toni Hopponen
Max Hoppy
Paul Hosford
Oksana Hoshva
Emma Houlton
Larisa Hovannisian
Marina Hramkova
Tony Hsieh
Cathy Hsu
Daniel Hu
Ching-Yun Huang
Lee-Sean Huang
Alexandra Huber
Tom Huges
Alex Hughes
Hector Hughes
Sebastiaan Hulst
Herve Humbert
Shane Hunt

Khuzema Hussain
Sabah Hussain
Rebecca Huxley
Bobby Hyam
Hasnain Hyder
Shehryar Hydri
Adam Hyslop
Alessandro Iacoponi
John Iley
Alasdair Inglis
Paul Irwin
Raishma Islam
Gabriel Isserlis
Daniel Ivanov
Angela Jackson
David Jackson
Seth Jackson
Tim Jackson
Britta Jacobs
Kyla Jacobs
Nyall Jacobs
Oliver Jacobs
Yarden Jacobson
Mark Jacobstein
Magda Jagielska
Amit Jaiswal
Christian Jakenfelds
Stefan Jakubowski
Allisyn James
Pip Jamieson
Omar Jamil
Matthew Janes
Mark Jarecki
Jothi Jayadevan
Joel Jeffery
Molly Jeffery
Dan Jefferys
Bart Jellema
Cameron Jenkinson
Simon Jenner
Jason Jeon
Andrew Jervis
Matic Jesenovec
Jimmy Jia
Annabelle Jiang
Tanya Jimale
Megumi Jinno
Frederic John
Nnenna John
Daniel Johnson
Matt Johnson
Robert Johnson
Sam Johnson
Molly Johnson-Jones
Chris Johnston
Charlie Jones
Kathryn Jones
Matthew Jones
Michael Jones
Nick Jones
Simon Jones
Alexander Jordan
Darren Jordan
Maneesh Juneja
Dorota Kabała
Elizabeth Kaelin
Raghavendra Kalakonda
Bhavini Kalaria
Liliya Kalashnik
Max Kalis
Kelly Kampen
Shri Kanagasabapathy
Steven Kandola
Antoni Kaniowski
Sithan Kanna
Prasanna Kannan
Chaida Kapfunde
Nishant Kapoor
Daianna Karaian
Steve Karminsky
Artur Karwatka
Kulsoom Kausher
Anita Kavaja
Claire Kavanagh
Koosha Kaveh
Alexander Kayser
Greg Keane
Hamilton Keats
Ezra Kebrab
Maja Kecman
Dan Keegan
Steve Keegan
Elizabeth Keen

Ben Keene
Jonathan Kellar
Paul Kelley
Katie Kelly
Liam Kelly
Declan Kennedy
Linda Kennedy
Helen Kensett
Ruth Kent
Endaf Kerfoot
Ausrine
Kersanskaite
John Kershaw
Songya Kesler
Mike Kevina
Nick Keynes
Sudarat
Khamsalee
Azeem Khan
Babar Khan
Hadia Khan
Haroon Khan
Usama Khan
Viktoria
Khechumyan
Sajjad Khoshroo
Lina
Khrystoforova
Ashot
Khudgaryan
Cassius Kiani
Andrew Kidd
Ashley Kienzle
Herb Kim
Min Kim
Danny King
Donald King
Fiona King
Raymond King
Howard Kingston
Rose Kinsella
Daniel Kirby
Robert Kirkwood
Tim Kitchin
Henryk Klawe
Kevin Kleber
Kelly Klein
Alexander Knapp
Duncan Knight
Ricky Knox
Andrew Ko
Michael Kohn
Wolf Kolb
Jacek Kolodziejski
Hector Kolonas
Dariusz Koltko
Michal Kopec
Elena Koronotova
Dominika
Korycka
Sara Koslinska
Tatiana Kostanian
Adam Kostick
Matti Kotsalainen
Desmond Koval
Shierley Koval
Marek Kowalczyk
Antonina
Kozerovskaya
Michał Kozioł
Jakub Koźniewski
Annette Kramer
Matthias Krampe
Lars Kremkow
Gregory Kris
Tom Kristensen
Magdalena Kron
Jessica Kruger
Jan Kruyt
Marta Krzeminska
Paweł Krzywicki
Kate Kubiak
Gregory Kubin
Agnieszka
Kuczynska
Abhishek Kumar
Anand Kumria
Paweł Kustosz
Nyasha Kuwana
Joyce Kwong
Karen Kwong
Tony Kypreos
Elena Lapina
Tomas Laboutka
Tadas Labudis
Harry
Lachenmayer
Mawuli Ladzekpo
Michael Lagau

Rachel Lai
Tiina Laiho
Waleed Lakhani
Sai Lakshmi
Dimple Lalwani
Katharine Lamont
Frank Lampen
Christophe Lamy
Daniel Land
Kristina Langhein
Benjamin Lanyado
Jeremy Larsson
Bharat Las
Noureddine Latrech
Humphrey Laubscher
Conall Laverty
Sam Law
Jude Lawrence
Seth Lawrence
Jonathan Lea
Charles Leach
Adam Leadercramer
Kylie Leavitt
Jakub Lebuda
Aideen Lee
Andrew Lee
Jeremiah Lee
Philip Lee
Susie Lee
Sam Lehane
Kim Leitzes
Lou Lemaistre
Frank Lemos
Maria Leon
Valeria Leonardi
Dan Lester
Suzannah Lester
James Lethem
Grace Letley
Gaby Levene
Enrico Levi
David Levine
Nick Levine
Jaka Levstek
Christopher Lewis
Eddie Lewis
Neil Lewis
Phil Lewis
John Li
Katherine Li
Pearl Li
Catherine Liao
Adtiana Lica
Jeremy Liddle
Daniel Lieberman
Brian Lim
Judy Lin
Lesley Lindberg
Sandy Lindsay
Alexander Linenko
Aleksandra Litorowicz
Josh Liu
Andrea Lo
Thato Loate
Greg Lockwood
Joseph Lockwood
Stuart Logan
Paolo Lombardi
Javier Lomeli
Alan Long
Kylie Long
Roger Longden
Tim Longman
Peter Longworth
David Lonngren
Jen Loong
Anna Loskiewicz
Samantha Lott
Rebecca Lovell
Matt Lovett
James Lowery
Jerry Loy
Leticia Lucero
Tomasz Luchowski
Adriana Lukas
Raoul Lumb
Fiona Lumsden
Christina Lundberg
Terry Lurie
Alexander Lushnikov
My Ly
Keith Lynn

Elia Lyssy
Aleks Malchrzyk
Rui Ma
Ricardo MacArio
Iain MacAuley
Brendon MacDonald
Bruno MacHado
Angus MacKay
Christina MacKay
Al MacKin
Julia MacMillan
Martin MacMillan
Tes MacPherson
Sylwester Madej
Gustavo Madico
Srin Madipalli
Paolo Maffei
Stanisław Magierski
Nick Magliocchetti
Olivier Magnin
Greg Maguire
Mehul Mahatma
Amar Mahboob
Michael Maher
Nadia Mahmoud
Yasmine Mahmoudieh
Stefano Maifreni
Natalia Majcher
Katarzyna Majgier
Alistair Malins
Sarah Maloof
Sarah Malter
Dariusz Mankowski
Anthony Mann
Emma Marashlyan
Daniel Marczak
Marcin Marczyk
Zara Marin
Sebastien Marion
Ganna Markarova
Maria Marklove
Shane Marks
Etienne Marleau-Rancourt
Stefano Marrone
Chris Marsh
Nick Marsh
Ruth Marshall-Johnson
Nick Martin
Nicolas Martin
Sean Martin
Tommaso Maschera
Adam Maskell
James Maskell
Tatiana Maslennikova
Tshepo Mathabathe
Mayank Mathur
Johnathan Matlock
Terence Mauri
Ian Maynard
Hugh McNulty
Mannix McAlister
Nigel McAlpine
Mark McCaigue
Chris McCarthy
Cormac McCarthy
David McCarthy
Dot McCarthy
Byron McCaughey
Lisa McCausland
Rob McCombie
Ryan McDaid
Patrick McDermott
Kevin McElroy
Dani McFerran
Stewart McGowan
Kevin McGrath
Ciaran McGuinness
Jamie McHale
Tyvand McKee
Alicia McKenzie
Emma McLaren
Lee McLaughlin
Logan McLean
Stan McLeod
Nikki McMahon
Rory McMillen
Aaron McNeilly
Hugh McNulty

Owen McNulty
Cooper
Katie McPhee
Alex McPherson
Paul McQuade
Daniel McRitchie
Alasdair
McWilliam
Lachlan
McWilliam
Annabel Meagher
Fromme Mee
Frank Meehan
Shankar Meembat
Anna Meliksetyan
Justin R. Melville
Robert Mendel
Juliana Mendez
Marian Mentrup
Ian Merricks
James
Merryweather
Ali Meruani
Luigi Meschini
Alex Metelerkamp
Mandeep Metharu
Juliana Meyer
Richard Meyer
Kevin Meynard
Rafael Meza
Christian Miccio
Alistair Michener
Blake Micola
Alan Midgley
Magdalena
Miernik
Martin Mignot
Chris Mihos
Norbert
Mikołajczyk
Judith Millar
Scott Millar
Edward Miller
Fergie Miller
Matt Miller
Paul Miller
Sheryl Miller
Denise Mills
Rich Mills
Alex Milne
Richard Milnes
Tiernan Mines
Komal Mirza
Luke Miskelly
Blake Mitchell
Julia Mitchell
Keren Mitchell
Adam Mitcheson
Zahid Mitha
Rudradeb Mitra
Hrishi Mittal
Nhlanganiso
Mkwanazi
Bongani Mngadi
Asari Mohamath
Nicholas
Monnickendam
Dean Moon
Jeff Moore
Jody Moore
Shokoufeh Moradi
Matthew Morgan
James
Morgenstern
Tomio Morguchi
Tomokazu
Morisawa
Michelle Morris
Phat Morris
Quinton Morris
Samara Morris
Tony Morris
Jim Morrison
Karina Morrison
Kathryn Morrison
Carley Morrow
Karen Morton
Paul Mosley
Shauna Mounsey
Andrea Moustacas
Matt Mower
Fleurette Mulcahy
Avis Mulhall
Macartan Mulligan
Laura Vanessa
Munoz

Alina Muñoz Guirado
Steve Munroe
Peter Murane
Martin Murphy
Nuala Murphy
Rachel Murphy-Rutland
Jez Murrell
Eric Mushel
Steve Mushero
Felix Mussell
Ahmad Mustafa
Adam Muszyński
Luka Nachbar Cvikl
Alexandra Najdanovic
Cyrille Najjar
Greg Nance
Милан Nankov
Tarini Naravane
Binbin Narkprasert
Angela Nash-Blackwell
Nadia Naviwala
Francesco Nazari Fusetti
Moe Nazariha
Vitaly Nechaev
J. Paul Neeley
Lindsay Nelson
Nick Nettleton
Thorsten Neumann
Tom New
Laura Newbold
Alan Newman
Chris Newman
Jeremy Newman
Melissa Ng
Keyzom Ngodup
Yasmin Nguyen
Martin Ngwong
Richard Nicholas
Chloe Nicholls
Ross Nicol
Crispin Nieboer
Krzysztof Niebrzydowski
Tom Nielen
Georgie Nightingall
Julia Nikisena
Carla Nikitaidis
George Nindi
Vik Nithy
Paul Noakes
Suzanne Noble
Andrey Nogin
Peter Nolte
Anna Norman
Tim Norris
Ben Nottingham
Anna Nowak
Justyn Nowak
Ewa Nowakowska
Andrew Nowell
Jarek Nowotka
Adam Nowotny
Rodney Ntlemo
Abigail Nurock
John Nussey
Bettina Nyquist
Pádraig Ó Duinnín
Gerard O'Brien
Maurice O'Brien
Alex O'Byrne
Matthew O'Connor
Sam O'Connor
Louise O'Donnell
Miceal O'Kane
Chris O'Neill
Henry Oakes
Gareth Oakley
Sam Oakley
Martyna Obarska
Anisha Oberoi
Natalia Obolensky
Lisa OBrien
Todd OBrien
Manasseh Obura
Anthony Ogunbowale-Thomas
Leyla Okhai
Richard Oki
Murat Deniz Oktar
Andrzej Olejnik

Nadiia Tabaniuk
Oleksandrivna
Kjetil Olsen
Fope Oluleye
Charles Oneil
Michał Opiłowski
David Orman
Daniele Orner
Jody Orsborn
Carrie Osman
Jacek Ostrowski
Jude Ower
Konrad Ozdowy
Benjamin Ozsanay
Eylem Ozturk
William Page
Lisette Paget
Mark Palfreeman
Oliver Palmer
Ersin Pamuksuzer
Hector Pang
Lawrence Pang
Mike
Papageorgiou
Konstantinos
Papamiltiadis
Fiona Park
Sung Park
Andy Parker
Tom Parling
Ashkan Parsa
James Parton
Carl Partridge
Sylvia Pascoe
Tom Passmore
Malin Patel
Soul Patel
Rachel Paterson
Robin Patin
Nicholas Paul
Laura Paulekaite
Olga Pavlovsky
Jeff Pawlak
Samuel Payne
Xavier Paz
Charlotte Peace
Charlie Peacock
Marina Pearson
Nathan Pearson
Zoe Peden
Jasmine Pengelly
Desmond Penny
Rachel Peplow
Margaret Perchik
Sarah Percy-Davis
Alex Peretti
Jesus Perez Batlles
Valentyn Pertsiya
Tom Peters
Lorenzo Petrillo
Georgi Petrov
Julie Pham
Simon Philipp
Karen Phillips
Scott Phillips
Pavlo Phitidis
Judy Piatkus
Tom Pickersgill
Hugo
Pickford-Wardle
Ian Piggin
Stephen Pini
Phi Pinnell
Mark Pinsent
Nikolay Piriankov
Romain Pison
Elinor Pitt
Giulia Piu
Rich Pleeth
Elena Plescenco
Alexandra
Pluthero
Gevorg Poghosyan
Darion Pohl
Stevan Popovic
Thomas Portier
Simon Potter
Sarah Potterton
Isambard Poulson
Rahul Powar
Shona Power
Piotr Prajsnar
Jessica
Prawirohardjo
Lloyd Price
Jonathan Prince
Jan Prószyński
Ollie Purdue
John Purkiss

Sunil Purohit
Mark Purvis
Phillippa Pyatt
Mike Pye
Craig Pyser
Hasan Qasem
Catherine Qian
Chris Quickfall
Jennifer Quinn
Jamie Quint
Vijay Rabheru
George Radford
Hiten Radia
Abdulrahman
Rafiq
Keyan
Rahimzadeh
Bala Raju
Kunal Rajvanshi
Steven Ramage
Raj Ramanandi
Uj Ramdas
Toby Ramsden
Esther Raphael
Stephen Rapoport
Luke Raskino
Darren Ratcliffe
Stefan Raue
Tariq Rauf
Richard Rauser
Hemal Rawal
Mark Rayner
Urouge Raza
Carina Read
Charlie Regis
Daniel Reilly
Stan Reinholds
Seena Rejal
Alice Revel
Theresa Reyna
Alex Reynolds
Delissa Reynolds
Matthew Reynolds
Alexander
Rheeney
David Rhoades
Owain Rhys
Hughes
Alicia Ribas
Andre Ribeiro
Thomas Ribes
Nathalie Richards
Olly Richards
Frances
Rikard-Bell
Lauren Riley
Leo Rios Solis
Wolfgang Ritter
Andy
Rivett-Carnac
Louise Rix
Robert Rizea
Charlotte Roach
Matthew Roach
Simon Rob
David Roberts
Diane Roberts
Mark Roberts
Matt Roberts
Sebastian
Robertson
Graham Robinson
Josh Robinson
Simon Robinson
Mads Rode
Francis Rodino
Fred Roed
Simon Rohrbach
Roi Lustik-Cohen
Damian Rokita
Vincent Roman
Fab Rooke
Michael Rose
Shams
Rose-Mcnairn
Rodolfo Roseto
Meri Rosich
Felix Rossknecht
Francesco Rotilio
Carolyn Rowley
Caitlin Rozario
Asaf Rozin
Tamara Rubin
Jared Ruddy
Alicja Rudowska
Martin Rue
Rafael Ruiz
Weronika
Ruszecka

Tomas Ruta
Angate Ryan
Irene Ryan
Marie Ryan
Peter Ryder
Diana Ryduchowska
Federica Saccia
Pietro Saccomani
Saman Sadeghian
Ewa Sadowska
Magdalena Sadowska-Pożycka
Jose Saez
Ali Safari
Ahmad Saffi
Chandreyi Saha
Charlotte Salasky
Julia Salasky
Mauricio Salazar
Tom Samodol
Lourdes Sampera Tsukada
Sabina Samulska
Laura Sanchez
James Sandberg
James Sandoval
Kajal Sanghrajka
Thando Sangqu
Martin Santibanez
Afonso Santos
Edward Saperia
David Sargeant
Riham Satti
Christina Saunders
Julian Saunders
Martin Saunders
Tia Saunders
Natasha Savage
David Saxby
Mohsin Sayeed
Fani Sazaklidou
Yuliya Sazonenko
Adam Scales
Jordan Schlipf
Sebastian Schmitt
Jason Schoolmeester
Klaus Schottler
Pascal Schuele
Amanda Schulze
Piotr Schumacher
Alex Schwaderer
Simon Schwall
Michelle Sciama
Mateusz Ściechowski
Kate Scobell
Mike Scott
Paul Scott
Peter Secombe
Maia Segura
Tibor Sekelj
Joel Selvadurai
Przemek Sendzielski
Joan Senent
Zeynep Şener
Sarah Senior
Robert Sepulveda
Roudie Shafie
Amit Shah
Asma Shah
Hussain Shah
Rockwell Shah
Jonathan Shakhovskoy
Aniruddha Sharma
Darren Sharp
Alon Shats
Ashley Shaw
Ryan Shaw
Sam Sheckman
Troy Sheehan
Ben Sheeran
Chris Sheldrick
Damien Shiells
Sarah Shilling
Alpa Shingadia
John Shinnick
Kubair Shirazee
Kim Shore
Piers Shotter
Tatiana Shumilovich
Oliver Shurville
Henry Sidsaph
Anne Siew
Alex Siljanovski

Richard Silk
Joseph Silmon-Clyde
Roberto Simi
Matthew Simmonds
Alexander Simmons
Dan Simmons
Shed Simove
Gerrit Sindermann
Oojal Singh
Louise Sinnerton
Jeg Sithamparathas
Clarence Sittampalam
Tomasz Skalski
Agnieszka Skłodowska
Piotr Sklodowski
James Skowronski
Anna Skrobisz
Grant Slatter
Tom Slattery
Phil Slorick
Angelika Słowik
Sergiy Slupsky
Tim Smalley
Will Smelko
Garfield Smith
Krista Smith
Lynette Smith
Matt Smith
Simon Smith
Agata Smolich
Nicky Smyth
Noam Sohachevsky
Saeed Soheily
Artavazd Sokhikyan
Lara Solomon
Nick Soman
Alex Somervell
Danny Soos
Caroline Southwell
Macek Sowinski
Kerem Sozugecer
Tom Spalding
Wesley Spencer
Shashank Sripada
Luke Stahmer
James Stairmand
Mira Stammers
Dimitar Stanimiroff
Jerry Staple
Dave Stapleton
Kam Star
Henryk Stawicki
Martin Stead
Matthew Steans
Andrew Steele
Evan Stein
Alex Stephany
Ben Stephenson
Ed Stephenson
Edward Stephenson
Giorgia Sterza
David Stevens
Ben Stevenson
Catherine Stevenson
Dave Stewart
Eliot Stock
Jamie Stocks
Andy Stofferis
Simon Stokes
Atanas Stoyanov
Laza Stoynich
Maciej Straszewicz
Mark Stringer
Ingo Strobel
Jean-Baptiste Strub
Paul Sturrock
Jakub Styliński
Edric Subur
Weerada Sucharitkul
Alexander Suess
Mirela Sula
Ben Summers
Tim Summers
Steven Sun
Nicky Surangkhana
Nicky Surapaitoon

Siriporn
Surapaitoon
Alvise Susmel
Jon Sutcliffe
Sebastian
Sutherland
Darren Swanepoel
Matt Sweeny
Yael Swerdlow
Paulina Sygulska
Tom Sykes
David Symons
Lukasz Szafranski
Piotr
Szczepankowski
Paweł Szczęsny
Marta Szymanska
Tomasz Szymanski
Jakub Szymczyk
Nadiia Tabaniuk
Ben Tagger
Nicholas Taheri
Freddie Talberg
Seth Talbott
Natalia Talkowska
Christopher Tam
River Tamoor Baig
Eve Tamraz
An Shun Tan
Catherine Tan
Clara Tan
Bobby Tang
Damien Tanner
Joanna Tarnowska
Vesselina Tasheva
Tim Tasker
Aaron Taylor
Brian Taylor
Jason Taylor
Joy Taylor
Leo Taylor
Mark Taylor
Phil Taylor
Rebecca Taylor
Toyia Taylor
Will Taylor
Devika Thapar
Nick Theodore
Alasdair Thin
Brian Thomas
Chris Thomas
Jacob Thomas
Nick Thomas
Ken Thompson
Steve Thompson
Simon Thorpe
Ben Thrasher
Kes Thygesen
Christopher Tia
Adeline Tiah
Sarah Ticho
Grant Tickets
Lisa Tilley
Nathan Ting
Chris Tingley
Sri Kartina
Tjandra
Ksenia Tkacheva
Jamie Tolentino
Dominik Tomasik
Magdalena
Tomkowicz
Peter Townsley
Kelsey Traher
Mai An Tran
Peter Treacher
Alastair Treharne
Bastien Treptel
Francisco
Trindade
Maria Trokoudes
Yota Trom
Cate Trotter
John Troyer
Dawn Trudeau
Katleho Tsoku
Aleksandr
Tsukanov
Minh Tu
Poppy Tucker
Stephen Tucker
Steve Tucker
Charles Tugendhat
Eamon Tuhami
Maria Tulino
Ewa Tumanow

Davide Turi
Lee Turner
Mark Turner
Agata Twardowska
Mark
Twum-Ampofo
Deborah Tyfield
Eyal Tzabari
Mika Uehara
Siren Uludag
Emeka Umunna
Tim Underhill
Kelsey
Underwood
George Urdea
Eda Utku
Paolo Valdemarin
Amanda Vallis
Nicole Van Der
Bogert
Aline Van Der
Meulen
Alex Van Klaveren
Ryan Van Quill
Stefan Van Tulder
Jeroen
Vanderhaeghen
Paul Varga
Jolyon Varley
Nastasha Velasco
Lino Velev
Alexander Velkov
Kumy Veluppillai
Chris Verbick
Marja Verbon
Matthieu
Vermeulen
Will Verrill
Marta Vickland
Manuel Victor
Jarongrat
Vilainatre
Kat Vilainatre
Iryna Volk
Katarzyna Von
Alexandrowitsch
Thomas J. Vosper
Buddy
Waddington
Kavin Wadhar
Maria Wagner
Sven Wagner
Julian Wakefi eld
Jacek Walesiak
Jeremy Walker
Sophie Walker
Anna Walkowska
Fergus Wallace
Mark Wallace
Jozef Wallis
Patrick Walsh
Nicholas Walters
Mark Wane
Lisa Wang
Pin Wang
James Ward
Paulina Wardak
Kacey Wardle
Matthew Wardle
David Warren
Zuzanna Warso
Liz Warwick
Stephanie
Warzecha
Ben Waterman
Dan Watkins
Jamie Watson
Mark Watts
John Webb
Paweł Weber
Jonathan Webster
Phil Weiss
Andy Welsh
Jay Wen
Elise West
Katie Wheatley
Steve Wheen
Max Whicher
Tom Whicher
Liz Whitaker
David White
Jonny White
Oscar White
Richard White
William White
Andrew Whittaker
Jeremy Wickremer
Marlena
Wieczorek

Rob Wilcocks
Robert Wilcocks
Lech Wilczyński
Ben Wilding
Florian Wilisch
Chris Wilkins
Andi Wilkinson
James Wilkinson
Meryn Willetts
Darin Williams
David Williams
Lee Williams
Rick Williams
Ryan Williams
Sean Williams
Trevor Williams
Jess Williamson
Kelly Williamson
Nicole Williamson
Roger Willis
Lucy Wills
Marnie Wills
Daniel Wilson
David Wilson
Gian Wilson
Jamie Wilson
Jennifer Wilson
Kelvin Wilson
Richard Wilson
Sebastian Wilson
Charlotte Winslett
Gavin Wiseman
Michal Wisniewski
Sebastian Witalec
Melissa Witmer
Christopher Witt
Anja Witte
Tomasz Włodarczyk
Klaudia Wojciechowska
Piotr Wojciechowski
Grzegorz Wolański
Silke Wolf
Adrian Wong
Helen Wong
Vincent Wong
Liana Woo
Richard Wood
Tom Wood
Jon Woodall
Archie Woodhead
Daryl Woodhouse
Phil Woodward
Alexander Woolley
Emeline Wraith
Paul Wright
Martin Wroe
Brandon Wu
Joe Wu
Naree Wu
Sean Wu
Otto Wüst
Derek Wyatt
William Wynne
Tony Xhufi
Tony Xu
Tsung Xu
Sen Yang
Shaoming Yang
Olga Yanusik
Evelina Yasaveeva
Claire Yates
Viktor Yevpak
Thomas Yohannan
Jennifer Yorke
Chris Young
Daniel Young
Greg Young
Robin Young
Stuart Young
Will Young
Arry Yu
Kevin Yu
Mohamud Yussuf
Azmat Yusuf
Rebecca Yyc
Elizabeth Zaborowska
John Zaheer-Flaherty
Murtaza Zaidi
Denis Zakharenko
Nadim Zaman
Angelo Zanetti
Ruth Zannis
Manuel Zapata

Mariusz Zarzycki
Joanna Zawicka
Charlie Zazzera
Abby Zhang
Chao Zhang
Fan Zhao
Aimee Zheng
Valeriya Zhuk
Marc Zornes
Chenting Zou
Rui Zu

*This 'thank you' list is from a 9others Eventbrite extract and includes everyone who signed up through Eventbrite and attended a meal with 9others between 8 December 2011 and 31 December 2021. If we've missed anyone we're very sorry, but please let us know.

Reading list

If you're now itching for something else to read, then dive into these books we've selected. 9others for your bookshelf, if you will…

1. *How to have a happy hustle: The complete guide to making your ideas happen* by Bec Evans (2019)
2. *Anything you want: 40 lessons for a new kind of entrepreneur* by Derek Sivers (2022)
3. *The courage to be disliked: How to free yourself, change your life and achieve real happiness* by Ichiro Kishimi and Fumitake Koga (2018)
4. *What I wish I'd known when I was young: The art and science of growing up* by Rachel Sylvester and Alice Thomson (2022)
5. *The 'ShipIt' journal* by Seth Godin (available from: https://seths.blog/wp-content/uploads/2012/05/theshipitjournal.pdf)
6. *Unreasonable success and how to achieve it: Unlocking the nine secrets of people who changed the world* by Richard Koch (2022)

7. *The hard thing about hard things: Building a business when there are no easy answers* by Ben Horowitz (2014)
8. *Zero to one: Notes on startups, or how to build the future* by Peter Thiel (2015)
9. *Founders at work: Stories of startups' early days* by Jessica Livingston (2008)

Your favourite search engine will take you right to them.

Looking for more 9others content?

- Listen to our *Brilliantly Easy, Stupidly Difficult* podcast about the choices we make and the lives we end up living: https://9others.com/podcast
- Sign up to our email list: https://9others.com/news

About the authors

Katie Lewis

Katie Lewis has supported thousands of companies to raise investment in the UK and abroad. She is currently COO at a high-growth scaleup. What gets her up in the morning is the opportunity to bring people together in a supportive and trusting environment with 9others.

Matthew Stafford

Matthew Stafford is a connector, investor and trusted counsel to entrepreneurs around the world. As the co-founder of 9others he has personally hosted hundreds of 'meals with 9others'. Matthew invests via www.stafford.vc

Index

www.ingramcontent.com/pod-product-compliance
Ingram Content Group UK Ltd.
Pitfield, Milton Keynes, MK11 3LW, UK
UKHW021650091125
464885UK00002B/92

9 781805 417644